C000026476

HIDDEN HISTORY
of
CLEVELAND
SPORTS

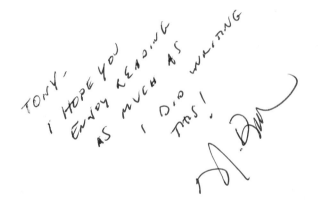

Tony -
I hope you enjoy reading as much as I did writing this!

A. Bona

MARC BONA

THE
History
PRESS

Published by The History Press
Charleston, SC
www.historypress.com

Copyright © 2021 by Marc Bona
All rights reserved

Front cover, top left: Georgia Tech Athletics; *top right*: author's collection; *bottom left*: Detroit Publishing Company via Library of Congress; *bottom right*: Nancy Stone, the *Plain Dealer*.
Back cover, top: Robert J. Quinlan, the *Plain Dealer*; *bottom*: Andrew Cifranic, the *Plain Dealer*.

First published 2021

Manufactured in the United States

ISBN 9781467146128

Library of Congress Control Number: 2021934328

Notice: The information in this book is true and complete to the best of our knowledge. It is offered without guarantee on the part of the author or The History Press. The author and The History Press disclaim all liability in connection with the use of this book.

All rights reserved. No part of this book may be reproduced or transmitted in any form whatsoever without prior written permission from the publisher except in the case of brief quotations embodied in critical articles and reviews.

For Lynne and Addie

CONTENTS

CONTENTS

PREFACE

So much has been written on The Fumble, The Shot, The Drive—ignoble moments in Cleveland's rich sports history. But there are under-the-radar, often forgotten individuals, teams and moments that deserve attention, set the scene or serve as milestones over many eras. Some have been mostly forgotten as the years pile on, while others were a passing glimpse in sports history.

Some of the subjects in this book were born in Cleveland. Some died here. All left a mark here.

As I researched this book, I found myself saying, "Hmm, I didn't know that." Or I might have known a fact or two about an era, team or player, but as I dug deeper I uncovered details that surprised me. Imagine taking a rock hammer and hacking repetitively until, all of a sudden, a small, shining gem appears. Constantly while I worked on this book, rabbit holes popped up. I would go down one, two or more, often in pursuit of one detail that might yield a sentence or two in a chapter. It didn't always work out. But it was always worth it.

The goal I tried to achieve is for anyone who picks up this book to have the same feeling reading it that I had writing it: to simply say, "Hmm, I didn't know that."

ACKNOWLEDGEMENTS

No matter how solitary an experience researching and writing a book seems to be, it truly is dependent on other people, and they deserve a hat tip.

No chapter was complete before my editor and wife, Lynne Sherwin, read it and offered smart comments. Her deft eye, as well as her attention to big-picture and fine details, saved me multiple times.

My agent, Anne Devlin, has been instrumental in working with me on a variety of writing projects, and I appreciate her support. My editors at The History Press, John Rodrigue and Rick Delaney, lent a communicative, guiding hand along the way.

John Heisman graciously took my call while he was watching an Ohio State football game. He helped with my inquiries about his famous namesake great-uncle's residence in Cleveland. Duey Graham, son of Cleveland Brown great Otto Graham, responded immediately when I contacted him about researching the 1940s Browns. Kevin O'Toole, Johnny Kilbane's great-grandson, also replied quickly in my inquiry about his famous boxing ancestor.

Rich Exner is a longtime colleague with whom we share at least two things: We once both received paychecks from United Press International, and we were both sports editors of our respective Big Ten college papers at the same time. He has covered just about everything in his career and is more deft at crunching numbers into readable prose than anyone I know. His cleveland.com weather database is a gold mine, helping me create an accurate setting for ball games over the years.

Chris Quinn, vice-president of content for Advance Ohio, my employer, was quick to allow me use of photographs from cleveland.com archives. The work from our many talented photographers over the years truly helped my chapters come alive.

Often, research led me to burrow into a rabbit hole, and it was the kind assistance of others who helped pull me out. Grand Central Publishing's Ivy Cheng and publicist Jimmy Franco were immediately helpful in connecting me with Clarence Clemons's cowriter and close friend, Don Reo. Likewise, Bill Robinson, director of the Office of Public Relations with the University of Maryland Eastern Shore, was incredibly helpful in sharing photos of Clemons. Jason Chaimovitch of the American Hockey League clarified a perplexing mystery surrounding the 1938 Syracuse-Cleveland game. Don Stoner, sports information director at Augsburg College in Minneapolis, shared a great photo of hockey players at the college in 1928. Dave Hanson and Jonathon Jackson confirmed a key point clearing up a fact-versus-fiction moment regarding the movie *Slap Shot*.

My pal Scott Longert, who has chronicled the history of the Cleveland Indians in his wonderful books, was a go-to source when my research ran into contradictions. He is always willing to offer helpful advice.

Speaking of go-to sources, the wonderful collection of biographical portraits from the Society for American Baseball Research is invaluable to anyone delving into the sport's history. Cleveland-area writer-editor Vince Guerrieri shares my love of baseball history and offers impeccable research and clear writing for his many topics, including his must-read 2020 SABR biography of George Steinbrenner. My many invaluable sources used for citation and confirmation also include baseball-reference.com for box scores and Case Western Reserve University's comprehensive Encyclopedia of Cleveland History.

Finally, should the reader find errors in my research, I take full blame and offer a sincere mea culpa.

I

THE CLEVELAND INFANTS

One and Done

In 1890, newspaper readers were treated to articles about three major leagues, the American Association (AA), the National League and the Players' League.

Cleveland did not have an AA team that year, though newspaper accounts regularly included box scores and summaries. The National League team, the Spiders, featured a rookie named Cy Young. And then there were the Infants.

Cleveland's team played in the upstart Players' League (PL), which consisted of eight teams, including Boston, Brooklyn, Buffalo, Chicago, New York, Philadelphia and Pittsburgh. The league would last only one season. Cleveland finished 55-75. It counted the league's batting champion among the wide-ranging characters on the roster. One broke into the league when he was sixteen. Several hold major-league records. One died just months after the season ended. Another ended up in the Hall of Fame, a player whose death would be forever listed as mysterious. One player was once arrested during a game, while another created a lasting baseball tradition.

The Brotherhood of Professional Base Ball Players had been formed in 1885 as a response to strict limits imposed in the National League. Those limits included a salary cap and, most important, the reserve rule, which contractually bound players to a team. What the Brotherhood did for the short term was create a player-driven league. What it did for the long term was give birth to the notion of free agency. While it would be eighty-five years before free agency would be ingrained into the game, the Players' League in 1890 saw the athletes control their destiny.

The Delahanty family plot is in Calvary Cemetery in Cleveland. *Marc Bona.*

Star players jumped from established leagues to sign with Players' League teams. Hall of Famers King Kelly, Ed Delahanty, "Old Hoss" Radbourn, Pud Galvin and Deacon White all competed in the PL.

The league was the brainchild of John Montgomery Ward. It was born out of Ward's frustration with and opposition to the reserve clause, which shackled players in a system that created what amounted to indentured servitude. A player was strictly bound to his contracted team in an era that saw no agents, no union, no incentive clauses and no option years.

Ward was smart and a gifted athlete. He was a pitcher-turned-shortstop who became a lawyer. Ten years before the Players' League, Ward threw the second perfect game in major league history. In 1885, the year Ward created the Brotherhood of Professional Base Ball Players, he also earned his law degree.

So the Players' League entered the 1890 season filled with promise and hope for a long life, but it would flame out after just one season. Its teams had names like Quakers, Burghers and Wonders. Cleveland's entry in the league was the Infants.

Cleveland's roots in professional baseball date to the 1860s, with several incarnations of teams that danced their way into the history books. But dive into the backgrounds of players who jumped to the Players' League for what turned out to be a one-year sabbatical, and there often is scant mention beyond the obvious.

Even the genesis of the team's nickname is given passing reference. Often, teams were referred to in newspaper accounts by the plural of their city, like "the Clevelands." Robert N. Ross, who wrote *The Great Baseball Revolt*, says he is unsure of the origin of the Infants nickname and that "Virtually none of those late 19th-century teams had official names. They were usually incorporated using only their city and the league name in their legal papers. Any name beyond that was really a nickname, something fans and/or the press would call them based on a variety of factors."

Streetcar magnate Albert Johnson owned the Infants. A decade later, his brother Tom would begin serving the first of three terms as Cleveland's mayor. Tom Johnson also invented a coin-operated fare box that remains in use. (Even Albert Johnson's lengthy obit in the *Plain Dealer* in 1901 would only touch on his brief ownership of the team, focusing more on his streetcar business.) Albert was a player's owner and fought for the league. Years later, he would even hire Ward to represent his company when lawsuits were filed against Johnson's rail line in Brooklyn, New York.

While Johnson and his family were not Cleveland natives, their business was critical to owning a baseball team in the city. Fans needed a way to get to the park, and Johnson's streetcars were the perfect vehicle.

Cleveland's team played at Brotherhood Park, located at Willson Avenue, which would become the thoroughfare East Fifty-Fifth Street, and the end of Diamond Park. It was adjacent to the Nickel Plate Railway and streetcar terminals and easily accessible to downtown.

Cleveland opened the season at Buffalo, getting drubbed, 23–2. The team had some pop in its bats but was less stellar from the mound. Six of the eight starting position players hit .292 or higher, yet only one in four pitchers in the rotation had a winning record.

That is due in part to rule changes at the time. As baseball historian John Thorn notes:

In its attempt to win fan favor through increased scoring, the rival major league moved its pitching box back 1.5 feet and, with the addition of a new lively ball, produced a batting average twenty points higher than those in the two established major leagues. The 1890s were a hitter's heyday. Pitchers throwing breaking pitches at the new distance tired more quickly than their predecessors of the 1880s had; staffs now typically featured three and sometimes four starters where two had sufficed in the 1880s and one had been enough in the 1870s.

It was a year of highs and lows for Cleveland. On April 19, the team gave up twenty-three runs against Buffalo, the league's doormat. But the Infants scored twenty runs on June 2 against Chicago. Cleveland would finish in seventh place.

As was common in that era, the box scores only scratch the surface of the reality of this collection of players. But that's where things get interesting.

The irony behind Ed Delahanty was that he was born in Cleveland, yet 1890 was the lone season he played in his hometown. He would hit .346 over sixteen major-league seasons and wind up in the Hall of Fame. Despite holding the fourth-highest batting average of all time, he remains known for the circumstances surrounding his death rather than for his on-the-field accomplishments.

Delahanty, one of five baseball-playing brothers, could run, hit and field. And, like many ballplayers of the day, he could drink. Excessively.

On June 25, 1903, with the Washington Senators, he played in Cleveland in what would be the final game of his career. He traveled with the Senators to Detroit, then abandoned the team and left clothes in a hotel. With money and jewels on him, he boarded a train for New York but reportedly became drunk and boisterous and was ordered off near Niagara Falls.

Newspapers incrementally followed Delahanty's disappearance. A *Plain Dealer* account read:

> *The Washington club has been unable to locate Ed Delahanty, who suddenly slipped away from the club in Detroit last Thursday while the players were at the game and not a word has been received by any one as to where he is or what might have happened to him. He had not been taking care of himself and was not in the best mental condition the last seen of him, and considering the fact that he talked of suicide and that he left all his belongings at the Detroit hotel, it is feared the big fielder has taken his life. His wife is here [Cleveland] awaiting him and is greatly distressed because of her husband's strange actions.*

Lack of attribution aside, the brief account would turn out to be an accurate one, though some speculation exists that he was killed.

Delahanty's body was found on July 9, 1903. A leg was severed, reportedly from the *Maid of the Mist* touring boat's propeller.

Ed Delahanty's simple tombstone lies in his family plot in Calvary Cemetery in Cleveland. *Marc Bona*.

When he died, he was a seasoned veteran at thirty-five years of age. But in 1890, Delahanty was a twenty-two-year-old playing in only his third major-league season. He hit .296, surprisingly good for only fifth best on the team.

After Delahanty's death, sportswriter Robert Smith wrote this about the slugger in the *New York Times*:

> *Men who met Ed Delahanty had to admit he was a handsome fellow, although there was an air about him that indicated he was a roughneck at heart and no man to temper with. He had that wide-eyed, half-smiling, ready-for-anything look that is characteristic of a certain type of Irishman. He had a towering impatience, too, and a taste for liquor and excitement. He created plenty of excitement for opponents and spectators when he laid his tremendous bat against a pitch.*

Delahanty, who became the second major leaguer to hit four home runs in a game, drew praise from his Cleveland manager, Patsy Tebeau, who once said: "The most dangerous thing to throw that bat-mad galoot is a wild pitch. If you let him get a step into the ball he'll knock the cover off."

But in the end, as a SABR biographical portrait describes him, Delahanty's life was "ended abruptly by high living and low judgment."

Teammate Pete Browning also was a troubled soul, having been afflicted with mastoiditis, a bacterial infection in cells surrounding the ear. It caused serious discomfort, led to Browning self-medicating with alcohol and, eventually, his brief committal to an insane asylum. "In short," his SABR bio reads, "the mastoiditis was responsible for all his personal and professional problems."

Browning led the Players' League, hitting .373. He would finish a thirteen-year career with a .341 average, tenth best all-time. Fans who made their ways on

Pete Browning died at age forty-four. *Louisville Slugger Museum and Factory Archives.*

Johnson's streetcars to watch Cleveland in 1890 didn't realize it would be the sole season for the team or that two of its players would finish in the top ten batting averages of all time.

Like Delahanty, Browning would wear a Cleveland uniform for only one season. The men shared another trait: Each would be known for an off-the-field occurrence. With Delahanty, it was his mysterious death. Browning's name would be etched in baseball history.

Browning initially played for his hometown team, Louisville of the American Association. In a game in 1884, a slumping Browning reportedly broke his bat. (It should be noted that while any player can slip into a slump, Browning finished 1884, his third big-league season, hitting .336.) At the game was John Andrew "Bud" Hillerich, the seventeen-year-old son of J. Frederick Hillerich, who owned a woodworking shop. Junior supposedly convinced Browning that he could make a bat for him.

The story might be apocryphal, although Hillerich Jr. had played ball and made bats. Browning, as the story continues, tallied three hits the day after the teen gave him the newly made bats. In a quintessential American success story, it was the apprentice son who had to convince his set-in-his-ways father that this newfangled idea of making bats was the way to go. As the company's website proudly declares: "Despite Browning's teammates flooding to the Hillerich shop for bats, Bud's father saw a very different

Pete Browning hit .373 for the Cleveland Infants of the Players' League in 1890. He had forty doubles among his 184 hits. *Louisville Slugger Museum and Factory Archives.*

future for the company in stair railings, porch columns and swinging butter churns. At times in the 1880s, he actually turned away professional ball players seeking new bats. But Bud persisted and, after some time, his father relented to his son's unyielding enthusiasm." Ten years later, Bud took over the family business. The name *Louisville Slugger* was registered with the U.S. Patent Office.

So, more than 135 years later, it's Browning's name, of sorts, that lives.

Jim McAleer isn't a household name, but he, like Browning, did something years ago that lives on in baseball history.

McAleer, who was born in and buried in Youngstown, spent eleven of his thirteen major-league seasons with three teams in Cleveland: the

Spiders of the National League, the Blues of the American League and the 1890 campaign in the Players' League. McAleer, a light-hitting but stellar defensive centerfielder, hit .253 in his career. In 1902, he became the first manager of the St. Louis Browns in their inaugural season. They would finish 78-58, good for second place and five games back. That pioneering year would be his best in eleven years as a manager, including a stint guiding the Washington Senators, who finished in seventh place in 1910 and 1911. It was in Washington that he left his mark.

While there are some conflicting reference points, it appears that McAleer gets the credit for suggesting that President William Howard Taft throw out the first ball on Opening Day, April 14, 1910. According to Martin Stezano, writing for History.com, umpire Billy Evans, later a front-office executive with the Cleveland Indians, gave the ball to Taft. Walter Johnson would catch it.

The president took the sphere in his gloved hands as though he was at a loss what to do with it until Evans told him he was expected to throw it over the plate when he gave the signal. He handed the ball to Mrs. Taft, who weighed it carefully in her hand while the president was doffing his bright new kid gloves in preparation for his debut as a baseball pitcher. The president watched the players warm up and a few minutes later shook hands with the managers, McAleer and [Connie] Mack. When the bell rang for the beginning of the game, the president shifted uneasily in his seat, the umpire gave the signal and Mr. Taft rose, pulled his derby hat well down on his head, gave his blue serge trouser an extra hitch, gathered himself, drew back his arm and after a slight pause, threw the ball. Catcher [Gabby] Street stood at the home plate ready to receive the ball, but the president knew the pitcher was the man who usually began business operations with it, so he threw it straight to pitcher Walter Johnson. The throw was a little low, but the pitcher stuck out his long arm and grabbed the ball before it hit the ground.

Johnson would be savvy enough to send it to the White House and have it autographed. A day later, it was returned to him with the inscription, "To Walter Johnson with hope that he may continue to be as formidable as in yesterday's game. William H. Taft." Johnson did continue to be formidable; he won 417 games over twenty-one seasons.

Since that day, every president has thrown a ceremonial first pitch, though Jimmy Carter is the only president not to have done it while in office.

While McAleer would go down in history as being responsible for presidents throwing baseballs, Pop Snyder would be known for not catching them.

Snyder, who at thirty-five was the oldest player on the 1890 team, was known as a smart catcher. But his line in record books is an ignoble one. He holds the major-league mark for most passed balls in a career, 763. To be fair, and to keep eras in perspective, Snyder played at a time when dusk was both a batter's and a catcher's enemy. Catchers' fingers were gnarled into crooked claws from repetitive injuries. Mitts were in their infancy, little more than tiny pieces of padding sewn together. In fact, an early patent on a catcher's mitt didn't take place until 1889, and the more modern, rounded "pillow-style" mitt wasn't created until 1899.

It is unlikely that any club today would retain a .235 hitter for very long. But Snyder was known as a "backstop with brains" and is credited with creating a system of signals that became the forerunner of the game's "sign language," baseball historian Larry R. Gerlach writes.

Snyder played only thirteen games with Cleveland in 1890, but his name kept appearing in box scores. That's because the catcher became an umpire in the same season in the same league, unfathomable today. Regarding a game in September, the *Plain Dealer* wrote, "The crowd was extremely noisy and at times boisterous, calling Snyder, an old Cleveland favorite, all sorts of names."

Cub Stricker was an old favorite of sorts with Johnson. The ballplayer and the businessman were "secretly monitoring the city's [Cleveland] National League turnstile so that they could estimate their potential market," Robert B. Ross writes in his book about the Players' League. The two also were Cleveland's delegates to a key informational meeting in New York in November 1889.

STRICKER, 2d B., Clevelands

OLD JUDGE
CIGARETTE FACTORY.
GOODWIN & CO., New York.

Cub Stricker played for three Cleveland teams in his major-league career. *Benjamin K. Edwards Collection via Library of Congress.*

Johnson must have sensed a quality in Stricker to see him as a confidant. But as a player, Stricker had a reputation for being a bit rowdy.

Like McAleer, Stricker had played for all three Cleveland major-league teams during an eleven-year career. A dependable singles hitter (he played in 127 of 130 games in 1890, and 104 of his 133 hits were singles), Stricker owns a few trivial footnotes, both in and out of the box score.

In 1892, Stricker, a "notorious foul mouth," had his jaw broken by a poker-playing teammate. On August 5, 1893, while playing for Washington in his final big-league season, Stricker was arrested for his actions during a game.

With his team losing at Philadelphia in the sixth inning, Stricker chased a pop fly as the crowd jeered to rattle him. He was ejected but for some reason remained in the game. In the ninth inning, Stricker was arrested and briefly locked up. He met the accuser, William Wright, who had been hit "fair on the nose." Meanwhile, at the game, fights broke out in the stands. The charge against Stricker was rescinded.

Various accounts say Stricker, who was being heckled, had faked throwing the ball in the stands. After that sophomoric schoolyard prank, he then really threw the ball. He later claimed that he was aiming for the fence.

The incident wasn't the first time Stricker was arrested in connection with something that happened on a baseball field. In 1887, he was arrested and charged with playing ball on a Sunday when he was with the Cleveland Blues.

Stricker holds an infamous statistical achievement: having the lowest on-base plus slugging percentage (OPS) for players who have scored at least 750 runs. The statistic weighs a player's on-base percentage (how often a batter gets on base) with his slugging percentage (a measurement that values extra-base hits). Stricker's was .600. Compare that with Babe Ruth, who, at 1.1636, holds the top spot among all players in the OPS category.

While Stricker held the lowest batting average (.244) among the starting position players, Willie McGill was the only pitcher in the four-man rotation to finish the season with a winning record (11-9). And when McGill made his debut on May 8, 1890, he was sixteen. The youngest player in the majors today would be twenty or twenty-one, with an occasional nineteen-year-old finding his way into a lineup.

In McGill's first game, his first four pitches were balls. He allowed another walk, a sacrifice fly, a hit and two runs. But he settled in, and Cleveland beat Buffalo, 14–5. McGill also went 1-4 at the plate.

Here's how a *Buffalo Express* writer described him in the language of the day: "A young man named McGill, a regular Davy Force sort of ballplayers [very short], was in the box for Cleveland. He is like the little girl's definition of a sugar plumb, round and rosy and sweet all over, and he throws barrel hoops and corkscrews at the plate. Once in a while he varies these with a swift, straight ball that is as full of starch as though it had just come from the laundry."

McGill was born on November 10, 1873, in Atlanta, making him sixteen years, five months, twenty-eight days old when he took the mound for the first time. Pop Snyder, who caught McGill, was more than twice his age. One listing charting players' ages has McGill as one of about a dozen players ever to start a season at age sixteen. The record, of course, is held by Cincinnati's Joe Nuxhall, who was fifteen when he started a game in the World War II roster-depleted 1944 season. Nuxhall, though, was six feet, two inches, while McGill stood about five and a half feet tall.

McGill finished 71-73 over seven years but was out of baseball by the time he was twenty-two.

Larry Twitchell, who was born in and died in Cleveland, was the Shohei Ohtani of his day. A position player and a pitcher, he hit .263 over nine years while compiling a 17-11 record.

In 1887, while playing for Detroit of the National League, he went 11-1. In the loss, he allowed only one hit in a fourteen-inning game. On August 15, 1889, Twitchell became the first of ten players for a professional Cleveland team to hit for the cycle. He went six-for-six, scored five runs and amassed sixteen total bases. Three of his hits were triples. It should be noted that seven of the Cleveland Spiders playing in that game would jump to Cleveland's Players' League team in 1890.

It was in 1890 that Twitchell was involved in a rare move of being sent from one Players' League team to another. Midseason trades involving pennant contenders are common now, but the nascent league had what author Ross calls "the Buffalo situation." That team was struggling financially (a harbinger for the league's eventual demise) and had signed players of subpar caliber. An "emergency committee" was created, resulting in several players being sent to Buffalo. One was Twitchell. He was a position player for Cleveland; in Buffalo, he pitched, finishing the year 5-7. He hit .223 in fifty-six games for Cleveland, then .221 in forty-four games for Buffalo.

History would unveil sad fates for three of the players on the 1890 Cleveland team.

Sy Sutcliffe, who hit .288 over seven years, would finish the 1890 campaign with a .329 average, third highest on the team. In 1893, just months after playing his final game at age thirty, he died of Bright's disease, a fatal kidney

Left: Sy Sutcliffe had a great year in 1890 for the Infants. Tragically, he died three years later at age thirty. *Benjamin K. Edwards Collection via Library of Congress.*

Middle: Patsy Tebeau led the Cleveland Infants in 1890, his first managerial stint. He then managed the Cleveland Spiders for the next nine seasons. *Benjamin K. Edwards Collection via Library of Congress.*

Right: Paul Radford's best season was 1890. *Benjamin K. Edwards Collection via Library of Congress.*

disorder. (Hall of Famer Ross Youngs would die of the same disease at the same age in 1927.) Cinders O'Brien, one of the four pitchers on the 1890 team with one of the greatest names, went 8-16 with a 3.40 ERA. On March 11, 1892, he would die of pneumonia. His brief obit made a reference that he was slated to play that season for St. Louis. In a four-year career, he had 113 complete games out of 126 starts.

And Oliver Patrick "Patsy" Tebeau killed himself in 1918 in St. Louis. His wife was in Cleveland visiting family. He hit .298 on the 1890 team and picked up the managing duties toward the end of the season.

The other players on the team form a hodgepodge of personalities. Paul Radford's best season over a twelve-year career came in 1890, when he hit .292. Radford was a Sabbatarian. The denomination embraces Sunday as a day of rest. That belief affected his career, but not in 1890: The Players' League did not schedule Sunday games.

Pitcher Bill Gleason had one of the shortest careers with a cringeworthy statistical line, despite the optimistic note in the *Plain Dealer*'s advance of his first game.

Left: Pitcher Henry Gruber went 22-23 in 1890 for the Cleveland Infants. *Benjamin K. Edwards Collection via Library of Congress.*

Right: Jersey Bakley's losses put him in a class by himself. *Benjamin K. Edwards Collection via Library of Congress.*

The most interesting part of the game today will be the debut in the box of the new pitcher for Cleveland. His name is Gleason and like all new pitchers he is said to be a wonder. Gleason is a Cleveland boy and is one of the best of the many amateurs who have played in this city.... The youngster has all the curves and plenty of speed. President A.L. Johnson has great hopes that he will succeed and said last night: "If the young fellow doesn't become frightened he will fool someone."

Sounds promising? Here's what happened: Gleason traveled with the team to Buffalo and promptly allowed sixteen runs on fourteen hits in four innings. His ERA was 27. The only saving grace was that only six hundred people were at the park. Cleveland lost the game, 18–15.

Pitcher Henry Gruber had more success, winning twenty-two games. Unfortunately, he lost twenty-three. Like Gleason, Jay Budd played in only one game. A *Pittsburgh Post* writer was almost kind: "The extent of his batting was two foul flies which he watched falling with boyish glee." Budd became a horse-racing enthusiast before dying in 1923 of a heart attack in a Cleveland hotel. His brief obituary in Cleveland's *Plain Dealer* made no mention of his baseball career.

Jersey Bakley went 12-25 in 1890, but it was his overall body of work that puts him in an infamous category. He is, as the Society for American Baseball Research notes, the only pitcher to lose twenty-five games in a season in three major leagues—the American Association, Union Association and Players' League. He lost twenty games with the Cleveland Spiders in 1889.

Bakley didn't spend all his time on the mound. He actually filled in for umpires a couple of times in his career, including a July 1890 game after umpire Harry Leach had been knocked unconscious. Active players filling in for umps was not uncommon, thanks to the hazards of the day.

Charlie DeWald's brief baseball career was spent entirely with Cleveland in 1890. He went 2-0 late in the season and wound up in a retirement gig supervising Cleveland's cemeteries at $1,800 a year.

Finally, there was Henry Larkin, one of three players on the 1890 Cleveland team who hit for the cycle at some point in their career. Larkin was a productive player, hitting .330, and he managed the team for most of the season. But when he was replaced, it was noted with this weary and to-the-point comment in the *Plain Dealer*: "Larkin wasn't a good field captain and the change to Tebeau should have been made long ago."

That Boston won the sole PL pennant, or that Buffalo finished last, are footnotes in the annals of the game. Cleveland's Players' League team is often forgotten, largely because it was a blip in baseball history and because the game soon would settle into its two distinct, and current, established leagues. The Cleveland PL team outdrew its NL counterpart in attendance that year 58,430 to 47,478. Cleveland, though, had the lowest attendance in the Players' League.

While the players had sought control over their lives, backers did not have the financial stamina to stay in the game, and the Players' League folded. It was a one-year respite from the reserve rule, and many of the players would jump back into the other leagues. But for 1890, Cleveland remains a part of baseball history.

2

JOHN HEISMAN AND CLEVELAND

His name is attached to one of the most well-known and well-regarded trophies in all of sports, the honor going to each season's best college football player. Coach John Heisman was a vanguard of college football, coached in the most lopsided game in history and is remembered every year when the sport's best player is crowned with the trophy in New York. Its shape is just as iconic as the trophy itself: A facemask-less player strides, left arm cradling a football, right arm outstretched, warding off potential defenders.

Heisman led football programs at eight colleges in his career and revolutionized the game with a series of innovations still in use. And while fans may associate him with the trophy given in New York or his time at Georgia Tech, he was born in Cleveland.

In a prescient nod to the sport's future, John Michael Heisman was born the same year the first intercollegiate game was played: 1869. Heisman was born in Cleveland on October 23, and the game—Princeton at Rutgers—took place on November 6 of the same year. (Rutgers won with the very baseball-like score of 6–4.)

Heisman's father, Michael, settled in Cleveland among a wave of German immigrants in 1858, the year sewers were first laid in the city. He made barrels that held various liquids, including beer, for a company in Cleveland. Those suds being transported in barrels would act as a precursor for something else involving John Heisman many years after his death.

Heisman and his family eventually moved to western Pennsylvania as part of the movement of people who wanted to get in on the oil boom creating jobs and dreams. Michael Heisman did what he knew best—barrel making—and the business prospered. But before they moved east, the Heismans lived in what is now Ohio City, the neighborhood that sits just across the Cuyahoga River and formerly a rival in commerce to Cleveland. Here is where history becomes a bit murky. Bridge Avenue, an east–west street that cuts into the thoroughfare of West Twenty-Fifth Street, has a row of tidy homes crammed for a stretch. Sporadic businesses, restaurants and bars can be found among the small two-story houses. After research was conducted in the 1970s, civic groups lobbied for restoration of a home at 2825 Bridge Avenue, and on March 30, 1978, Cleveland City Council declared it a historic landmark. The problem is that the marker was at the incorrect address. A local judge who researched the address had determined that 2825 Bridge was the house. But he failed to note that after the turn of the century, many houses in Cleveland were renumbered. This came in part as a result of houses being built on lots between adjacent houses.

Heisman's birthdate also remains a question. The marker lists October 3, 1869, as the date of John Heisman's birth. A city births directory also lists that date, local historian Craig Bobby found. But the coach's great-nephew, who coauthored *John Heisman: The Man behind the Trophy* with sportswriter Mark Schlabach, writes that John was born on October 23, 1869. Coincidental confusion to muddy the facts might lie in Heisman's death date: October 3, 1936.

Many addresses over the years have been associated with Heisman, most of which are on Bridge Avenue. A story by Thomas Andrzejewski in the *Plain Dealer* suggests several addresses associated with Heisman. One theory says the home would have been located near the one with the marker, at what was then 183 Bridge, with the barrel business at 187. Other research says Michael Heisman paid property taxes on land and buildings at 4006 and 4008 Bridge through Lord & Barber, an early realty company founded by two of the first mayors of Ohio City. Research suggests one might have been Michael Heisman's barrel business and the other the family home. Inspections date the home construction to the latter part of the nineteenth century, though; whatever house Heisman was born in might have been razed and rebuilt.

Adding to the litany of addresses is one recounted in Heisman's biography, which suggests the family at one time lived at 59 Frankfort Avenue. Like Bridge Avenue in Ohio City, this street remains today, though it has been altered a bit. The house would have been located across the northwest corner of what is now Public Square, albeit more than two dozen years before the Soldiers and Sailors Monument was erected.

Right: John Heisman, in 1919, at the end of his tenure at Georgia Tech. *Georgia Tech Athletics*.

Below: An historic marker was put up in April 2021 at John Heisman's house at 3928 Bridge Avenue, in Cleveland's Ohio City neighborhood. *Marc Bona*.

Another source, cleveland101.com, which focuses on historic origins, says the 2825 Bridge location is wrong and suggests another address but offers no evidence.

> *The marker is not actually in front of the Heisman birth site. Due to a street number change, the marker was placed in front of the wrong house—the actual house on the location of his birth site is .4 miles away, on the opposite side of the road. Heisman's birthplace is at 3928 Bridge Avenue. The change of location is especially notable as the structure in question at 3928 appears to be the actual house that Heisman was born in, whereas the one that the marker is in front of was built at a later date.*

The 3928 house is what historian Bobby says is the correct address.

And on April 24, 2021, the efforts to rectify the inaccurate location culminated years of lobbying from residents and others, and a ceremony was held to mark the proper address.

After the move in 1874 to Titusville, Pennsylvania, where Michael Heisman joined the oil-boom hopefuls, John Heisman would go on to Brown University. On his train trip to Providence, he had a layover in Albany, and his love affair with the sport of football took hold. He had played a rudimentary version in high school, but here he saw the game at an elevated level. Heisman's playing career would not extend past college. A year after taking his law-school exams, he landed a job coaching at Oberlin College, fewer than forty miles southwest of Cleveland.

Heisman's coaching career is well documented and spans success at schools including Oberlin. On November 16, 1892, he led the Yeomen to a 16–0 victory over Case in Cleveland, believed to be his first game coaching in his birth city.

Two years later, while coaching Buchtel (now University of Akron), he guided his team to a 12–6 win over Ohio State, the only time any Akron team has ever beaten the vaunted Buckeyes.

It was with coaching that Heisman made his mark on football, mostly because of his innovative approach to the game. He essentially created the position of middle linebacker in 1892. He invented the snap from center we see today (though this appears to be out of necessity, since his quarterback at the time was six feet, four inches tall). He was a pioneer with signals, including "hike!" In 1903, Heisman's call for the legalization of the forward pass was rejected; he was simply a few years ahead of his time. He wanted the game split into quarters, developed padded uniforms and introduced the scoreboard (a nifty way for fans to see downs). In 1922, he suggested overtime rules that in their most basic form resemble what is used today. He also called for a playoff system.

As former Ohio State star Vic Janowicz, who won the 1950 Heisman Trophy, put it: "John Heisman was to football what Moses Cleaveland was to Cleveland. Every time you see a game you see Heisman innovation."

When Heisman's coaching career is examined, the famed 1916 Cumberland–Georgia Tech game is often mentioned. It's become more than a trivia question (What is the biggest rout in college football? Georgia Tech 222, Cumberland 0).

John Heisman coached at eight colleges during his career. *Georgia Tech Athletics.*

Much has been written on that mismatched blowout pitting a powerful Tech team, which would win a national title the following year, against a school that was in the process of disbanding its football program. Its impetus has been mulled over in the subsequent years: It was a revenge game for Cumberland running up the score that spring on Heisman's Georgia Tech baseball squad, which he coached. It served as a way to show Heisman's distaste for the practice of using points scored as a measurement in the rankings system of the day. And it was a point of closure in Heisman's coaching career. In 1903, his Clemson squad tied Cumberland in a conference championship game. Cumberland was awarded the title; Heisman went on to Georgia Tech.

It was at Georgia Tech that Heisman had his greatest success. He retired from coaching in 1927 and moved back to New York, where he and his wife had a home. In retirement, he became a fitness director at the Downtown New York Athletic Club. In 1935, he was put in charge of determining the criteria to honor the nation's best player with the Downtown Athletic Club Trophy. He did so reluctantly, believing football was a team sport. But he came around, and that year, the University of Chicago's Jay Berwanger won the award. Less than a year later, Heisman died. The award was renamed for him beginning in 1936, when Larry Kelley of Yale won. Cleveland serves as a bond between Kelley and Heisman: Kelley also is an Ohio native who left the state at a young age. He was born in Conneaut, seventy miles east of Cleveland and a stone's throw from Pennsylvania. At one point in his life, Kelley lived in Cleveland.

And while Heisman lived only briefly in Cleveland, another connection in the city serves as a bond with the famed coach: beer.

Many of the German immigrants settling in the city in the middle of the nineteenth century were brewers, and they opened breweries with the lagers they knew from their homeland. Beer was—and remains—near and dear to Clevelanders' hearts. (The state's craft breweries have been a burgeoning industry for several years.) And it seems that Heisman, in one way or another, was close to beer.

The address 59 Frankfort, which Heisman's great-nephew references in his book, was close to the Cleveland Faucet Company, which made "beer preserving faucets," which serve "as a valve to dispense beer on demand." The barrels Heisman's father made held beer, among other liquids. The possible addresses that Heisman lived at were very close or adjacent to cooperages his father might have owned. And more than one hundred years later, Heisman would be connected to beer in Cleveland in yet another way.

In Heisman's day, brewing began flourishing, and dozens of breweries popped up in the city. Through the wave of American business consolidation, many smaller breweries were gobbled up over the decades; for a brief, three-year period in the 1980s, there were no breweries. That is, until 1988, when Pat and Dan Conway founded Great Lakes Brewing Company on Market Avenue in Ohio City. It's about two blocks from Bridge Avenue and about three-quarters of a mile away from the home at 3928 Bridge Avenue, where Heisman was born. The brothers began brewing a type of lager called Dortmunder, a reference to the German city Dortmund and its unique, thirst-quenching brew. (To this day, compared to the array of beer styles being produced, it is not as common a style among American brewers.) The Conways initially decided to name it the Heisman but ran into legal issues.

"It's like a badge of honor for a lifelong customer to ask for a Heisman, because that indicates to the bartender that they've been coming to GLBC for over thirty years," Pat said.

So the coach's memory lives on in football and, in a more subtle and local way, beer. And the two Ohio schools where Heisman got his start in coaching also keep his name alive, albeit in different ways. A lodge built in 1934 in Heisman's name and formerly owned by the University of Akron, where he used to coach, had "fallen into deep disrepair" more than eighty years later. But in 2019, the university announced it was giving it back to the city, offering hope for future refurbishment and use. And Oberlin College still holds a John Heisman Club Dinner each fall.

A 1978 letter in the *Plain Dealer* notes Heisman's importance to Cleveland by citing sportswriter Hal Lebowitz, who called Heisman "our best kept secret."

3

BEFORE THE CAVS

The Cleveland Rebels and Frank Baumholtz

The Cavaliers played their first game in the NBA in 1970, but the history of the league in Cleveland goes further back.

The Cleveland Rebels took the court in 1946 as a member of the Basketball Association of America. That league would serve as the roots of the National Basketball Association. The NBA would then merge with the rival National Basketball League in 1949.

Teams come and go in fledgling leagues, and the Rebels lasted just one season. That season wasn't devoid of a few historical points and a goofy moment or two. Notable was the proliferation of Cleveland-area and Ohio athletes on the team. One star player, Frank Baumholtz, would go on to have a rich life off the court, but we'll get to him in a minute.

In 1946, the league consisted of eleven teams, with Cleveland in the five-team Western Division along with the Pittsburgh Ironmen, St. Louis Bombers, Chicago Stags and Detroit Falcons. The East was composed of the Providence Steamrollers, Boston Celtics, Toronto Huskies, Washington Capitols, Philadelphia Warriors and New York Knickerbockers.

The Rebels had a strong Cleveland presence. Cleveland-born Mel Riebe went to Euclid Shore High and College of Wooster and was a star on the Rebel team. He is believed to be the only College of Wooster player to have played in the NBA. Reserve Pete Lalich was born in Lorain, played for East Technical High School and went on to star at Ohio University. Bob Faught and Hank Lefkowitz went to Cleveland Heights High School. Northeast Ohio's outer regions also contributed to the roster. Ned R. Endress attended the University of Akron and later coached at St. Vincent and St. Mary High Schools, a merger of which resulted in a famous alumnus years later: LeBron James. Leo John Mogus went to Youngstown State and, like Riebe, is the only alumnus from his school to have played in the NBA.

"Big Ed" Sadowski went to high school in Akron and had a long career playing in assorted independent leagues. And Baumholtz is from tiny Midvale in Tuscarawas County.

Another player, Kenny Sailors, made a pioneering mark on the game. He invented the jump shot. Standing a hair under six feet, he worked on a one-handed shot. Sailors, who died at age ninety-five in 2016, was the last surviving member of the Rebels.

Interestingly, he was one of three University of Wyoming players on the 1946–47 Rebel team, along with Leon Brown and George Nostrand.

The team played at Cleveland Arena, which doubled as the home of hockey's Cleveland Barons. Located at 3717 Euclid Avenue, the arena was owned by Al Sutphin, who was part of a group that founded the Ice Capades. Sutphin, an Ohio-born sports promoter, also ran the Barons and Rebels.

The Rebels' inauspicious start came on opening night, when the boards forming the court atop the ice began to come apart, "revealing the patches of frozen water underneath." Sutphin reportedly kept the engineer and designer in the arena all night to figure out how to solve the board slippage. (It never happened again. Later, Sutphin said that four hundred bolts would be used to keep the boards in place. How that hardware could be used in boards that lock together atop ice was not explained.)

The Rebels weren't the only team to suffer initial bumps. Size-fourteen shoes could not be found for Washington center John Mahnken before his team's opener, forcing the big man to wear "moccasins" during the game.

Games were often double-billed with "prelims," matchups of local amateur or club teams before the Rebels took the court. (Where the amateurs dressed remains a mystery, as the Rebels and opponents would be in their respective locker rooms.) Reporters covering the Rebels often gave a sentence or two at most to these preliminary contests, which pitted teams like Blepp-Coombs, a sporting-goods store, against East Side Typewriters. One tilt even featured members of the Pittsburgh Steelers and Cleveland Browns, including Marion Motley, Lou Groza and Dante Lavelli.

Preliminary games weren't the only attraction Sutphin employed to put fannies in the seats. For the opener, George Bird's Musical Majorettes performed before tipoff. And anyone who was six feet, eight inches or taller got in free, a sometimes-used promotional tack and reference to six-foot, seven-inch Irv Rothenberg. Ads featured the figure of his "giant" height, thought to be an anomaly, to attract fans—ironic, as six feet, seven inches is much more average now in the NBA and never seen in the center position. Before one November 1946 game, a "foul line and long distance field goal shooting" contest pitted members of the Rebels and Capitols. One advertisement included the overstatement of "major league basketball" being the "World's Fastest Game."

And for this entertainment people plunked down $1.50, $2.00 or $2.40 a ticket to watch the Rebels, who wore light-blue uniforms with red-and-white trim at home and white uniforms with blue letters and numbers on the road.

The problem was that not many fans were heading to games. The Rebels averaged 3,100 in attendance, with a high being 10,263 for an exhibition against the New York Rens, a barnstorming Black team of the era, and a low of 182 (though that was during a snowstorm). They even tried matinee scheduling. In January 1947, they lost their sixth consecutive overtime game. Years later, the *Plain Dealer*'s Chuck Heaton would write that the "fans were noticeable only by their absence." (While basketball has evolved to the sport it is today, some things don't change in Cleveland: A brief announcement in the *Plain Dealer* in November 1946 instructed fans to be wary of a torn-up intersection at East Fortieth Street and Chester Avenue.) Also, none of the players in the Basketball Association of America were Black.

There were bright spots. A few weeks into the season, Leo Mogus set the league scoring record at 33, though that would be broken before season's end. In December, it was reported that the Rebels led the league in scoring, averaging 69.7 points per game. And they made the playoffs, although it was a fleeting postseason. After winning the first game of the best-of-three series at home, the Rebels lost to New York, two games to one. They were hampered by Riebe, who had a broken finger, and the absence of Frank Baumholtz. One of the Rebels' best players, Baumholtz had left the team to join the Cincinnati Reds.

Baumholtz was truly a two-sport star. He had played at Ohio University. The "apple-cheeked" standout helped his team reach the finals of the NIT. Baumholtz, on the losing team, was named MVP.

The year 1941 was huge for Baumholtz. After the NIT, Cincinnati Reds general manager Frank Lane signed him. (Later, Lane would unceremoniously earn the nickname "Trader Lane" after sending beloved slugger Rocky Colavito to Detroit in the most notorious trade in Cleveland Indian history.) After a brief stint playing for the minors, Baumholtz enlisted in the U.S. Navy in October. The attack on Pearl Harbor came two months later.

After college, Frank Baumholtz played professional basketball and Major League Baseball and served during World War II. *Ohio University Athletics*.

Eventually, he became a lieutenant and put in charge of a seagoing amphibious assault vessel in the Pacific theater supporting Allied landings at Iwo Jima and Okinawa. At one point, Baumholtz saw a kamikaze strike an American ship. Another time, a mortar shell ripped a hole through his ship moments before he walked by the area. He had limited medical training but, without a doctor aboard, occasionally was called to serve as a medic to stitch up soldiers.

"In times of stress you do things that on a normal basis you would never try to do and on a normal basis would be scared to death to do," Baumholtz said in an interview five years before he died. By the time he was discharged, he had earned a Bronze Star. Years later, his wife would wake him when he relived the war in fitful sleep. He was "fighting battles and directing traffic in what everybody had to do."

In 1946, he joined the Rebels and became the team's leading scorer. He played forty-five of the team's sixty regular-season games and averaged fourteen points per game. But in 1947—before the basketball season ended but also before Major League Baseball's season began—the Reds asked Baumholtz not to play basketball and to concentrate on baseball. Baumholtz had heard rumors that Sutphin was going to move the team to Providence. The Reds sweetened the deal with a check for several thousand dollars, and Baumholtz turned to baseball full time. In his final game with the Rebels, he scored fifteen points in a loss to St. Louis, and the team gave him a luggage set.

Here's the what-if scenario: If baseball had not been an option at the time and Baumholtz had finished the season, would the Rebels have advanced further in the playoffs? Would a possible championship have ignited any more passion in Clevelanders for basketball at the time? Would there have been a push for Cleveland to remain a part of the upcoming merger that formed the NBA?

Then again, Baumholtz did get that luggage set.

Days after the Rebels were eliminated, Baumholtz, an outfielder, was announced as a probable starter for the Reds in their home opener against St. Louis. He made his major-league debut on April 15, 1947, the same day as Jackie Robinson. Baumholtz went 2-4 with an RBI in Cincinnati's 3–1 win. Baumholtz would hit .283 and finish fifth in voting for Rookie of the Year (Robinson won it).

Despite Baumholtz's baseball career starting well, the Chicago Stags acquired the rights to the two-sport star for the 1949 season, but he did not sign. Instead, he was traded to the Chicago Cubs.

On September 28, 1952, the final day of the season, Baumholtz was unwittingly involved in what amounted to a stunt on the part of St. Louis Cardinal manager Eddie Stanky. With the Cardinals playing the Cubs, the skipper brought Stan Musial in from his centerfield position to take the mound against Baumholtz. Musial was about to earn the National League batting title, and Stanky wanted him to face Baumholtz, who had the second-highest batting average in the league. Baumholtz swung at the first pitch and got on base thanks to an error. It was the only time Musial pitched in his twenty-two-year Hall-of-Fame career, and it was the only time Baumholtz ever hit right-handed. Musial led the majors with a .336 average. Baumholtz finished second in the National League at .325. From all accounts, neither man liked the stunt.

Baumholtz finished his career with the Philadelphia Phillies in 1957. In all, he collected more than one thousand hits and finished with a lifetime average of .290.

Even with their two-sport star playing most of the 1946 season, the Rebels remain a footnote in the annals of basketball history. They finished 30-30.

Philadelphia—led by future NBA Hall of Famer Joe Fulks, who led the BAA in scoring—won the league's only championship. Less than two months later, on June 9, 1947, Al Sutphin pulled the plug on the Rebels.

Sailors would wind up with Providence. Riebe and Sadowski would go to Boston. The Rebels had two coaches: Dutch Dehnert started the season, then resigned and was replaced by Roy Clifford. Dehnert became a clerk at Aqueduct Racetrack in New York, a city where he had been a player years earlier. His replacement, Clifford, became an administrator in the Cleveland Heights–University Heights school system.

Several years later, Cleveland gave professional basketball another go, with the Cleveland Pipers. They are known mostly as the team that would launch George Steinbrenner's sports-team ownership reign. The Rebels and Pipers were merely setting the stage for the Cavaliers, who would begin play in 1970.

4

THE CREATION OF CHIEF WAHOO

In recent years, Opening Day in Cleveland meant more than baseball. It meant contentious showdowns outside the stadium over Chief Wahoo. The caricature represents a duality. For some, it remains an object of pride, nostalgia, a love of their Cleveland Indians. For others, it is a racist symbol and a reminder of oppression. But the logo didn't materialize overnight. Its origin goes way back, before the team was officially called the Indians. It evolved over time. How it came to be involves a couple of old-time ballplayers in Cleveland, a hockey team, a newspaper artist and a teenager from Cleveland.

As the story goes, in 1897, Louis Sockalexis, a member of the Penobscot tribe, made his major-league debut with the National League Cleveland Spiders. Even before the season, Sockalexis shined among the prospective players. In their first intrasquad game on April 2, manager Patsy Tebeau divided the team into the "Indians" and the "Papooses."

Sockalexis made his mark but flamed out after only three years, his Major League Baseball career cut short by alcohol abuse. The nickname would be revived, however, for the American League team almost twenty years later. Why a name was needed and why "Indians" was chosen can be traced to several players, a team owner and another team.

In 1910, Roger Peckinpaugh made his debut with the Indians. Peckinpaugh was born in Wooster but moved at a young age to Cleveland's East Side. He lived in the same neighborhood as Cleveland's star Napoleon

Lajoie. Peckinpaugh, known as a quiet leader, would become the youngest manager to lead a major-league team, at age twenty-three, for the New York Yankees in 1914. Peckinpaugh played in Cleveland for only parts of three seasons but returned to manage the team for seven seasons (1928–33 and 1941). Peckinpaugh had a reputation as a mature, steadying force for his teams, but he would have another influence on Cleveland years later. In his obituary in the *Plain Dealer* in 1977, it was said that he had resembled the Chief Wahoo caricature. "With his swarthy skin, dark eyes, great horn of a nose, jet black hair and beetling eyebrows, Mr. Peckinpaugh became a newspaper cartoonist's delight. Some think he was the inspiration for Chief Wahoo, the Indian emblem, first drawn as a hose-nosed brave by Fred Reinert of The Plain Dealer."

Being known as the Cleveland Naps (an homage to its star player-manager Lajoie) was fine—until Lajoie left town after the 1914 season. No Lajoie, no Naps. Team owner Charles Somers then called on several Cleveland sportswriters to create a name. What probably was on the minds of the writers and most baseball fans at the time was the 1914 Boston Braves. The Braves that year earned the tag "Miracle" preceding their nickname because of the team's phenomenal comeback in the second half of the season. Mired in last place on July 4, the Braves somehow surged and won the pennant running away, finishing ten and a half games ahead of the New York Giants. They then swept Connie Mack's Philadelphia A's in the World Series. (The next pennant the Braves won was in 1948, when they lost the World Series to Cleveland.)

The name for Cleveland's team actually was seen as being "temporarily bestowed" at first, but it stuck. The announcement in the newspaper was accompanied by a multitude of sketches of Indians with little sayings, one of which read, "Fellow fans: we've got the hunch that they're going to carry a real for sure Indian mascot!"

There's also a reference to the Boston Braves with the caption, "If the nature of the name has anything to do with pennant chances, they should cop the flag—for instance, look at the Boston 'Braves.'"

So the name was established, and assorted headdress logos not resembling what would become Chief Wahoo came into existence. Then, on May 3, 1932, the *Plain Dealer* ran a page-one sketch of an angry-looking, loincloth-wearing Indian running with an ax in his right hand and a knife in his left as an excited fan cheers him on. The team had just won its ninth consecutive game.

The sketch, "The Little Indian," was the creation of Fred Reinert, a thirty-one-year-old Clevelander who had served in World War I.

But it wasn't the first time Reinert had sketched an Indian in the pages of the paper. Cleveland had a hockey team called the Cleveland Indians from 1929 to 1934. The paper ran Reinert's sketches of stick-holding skating Indians, incorporating the caricatures with images of players in early graphics on the sports pages.

In 1939, the Indians' famed one-armed scout, Hugh Alexander, signed a young pitcher named Allie Reynolds. The Oklahoma native would make his major-league debut in 1942 and pitch five years for Cleveland before being traded in 1946 to the Yankees, where he spent the last eight years of his career.

Reynolds was part Muscogee (Creek) Indian. Multiple times in print he was called the "copper-skinned Creek." He became the first American League pitcher to throw two no-hitters in a season. "After the second one, Yankees broadcaster Mel Allen began calling Allie 'Super Chief,' a nickname that stuck," his Society for American Baseball Research biography reads. Reynolds was a consistent pitcher in his time in Cleveland and New York. The year 1946 would prove to be pivotal in the history of the Indian franchise: Bill Veeck led a group that bought the team. Reynolds was traded to the Yankees for Joe Gordon. And Veeck decided to hire the J.F. Novak Company to redesign the Indian logo. That task fell to a teenage draftsman named Walter Goldbach, who had attended Rhodes High School and who worked at his uncle's company on the West Side. Veeck's charge was a "cartoon-type character," and Goldbach was given "free rein" for his artistic creation. He ended up with "a picture of a smiling yellow-skinned Indian with a crooked nose, red feather and ponytail. Veeck loved it and it became part of the team's uniform in 1947, one year before the Indians won their last World Series." Goldbach received no extra compensation. (Incidentally, Goldbach has another tie to the team. His son is a stonemason who helped build Jacobs Field.)

It's clear that Novak took inspiration from Reinert's initial work in the *Plain Dealer*. The character already was "locally beloved," one researcher points out. Over the years, it morphed a bit—the face became redder, the eyes were tweaked—but it remained a "toothy grinning, hook-nosed, pony-tailed, red feather-clad caricature."

Years later, in an interview, Goldbach said it was pointed out to him that the mascot's one feather indicates he is a brave, not a chief.

It's not known when the character itself was officially tabbed "Chief Wahoo." In 1951, the *Plain Dealer*'s James E. Doyle introduced couplets in his sports column, quick two-liners that he signed off with "Chief Wahoo's-this." He penned this one the day after Bob Feller threw a two-hitter, facing only twenty-nine batters:

> *It's great to see Bob Feller show how*
> *He's mastered that old pitching know how.*
> —*Chief Wahoo's-this*

It was around this time that the character of Chief Wahoo began showing up at events like school fundraisers. Doyle's doggerel ran for more than twenty years, ending in 1974.

Two years before Doyle's final verse appeared in print, Native Americans sued the Indians about the logo, claiming it was "degrading, demeaning and racist." Other lawsuits would come and go.

But Wahoo remained ingrained with fans. For the September 8, 1989 game at Cleveland Municipal Stadium, the Cleveland Regional Transit Authority and the Indians, in a joint promotion, offered a deal for fans to ride free to the game if they showed the driver the logo on anything—cap, shirt, pennant, whatever. It also included a half-off ticket coupon. That night, 13,489 fans showed up to see Cleveland beat Toronto, 5–4.

A year later, Jim Tomasewski wrote a letter to the *Plain Dealer* calling for a new logo. "While the media, both print and broadcast, local and national, have editorialized against all forms of racist behavior, none demonstrates the least bit of concern about offending anyone with the image of Chief Wahoo in sports reports." In 2000, Mayor Michael White denounced Chief Wahoo as racist and "proposed stripping the Cleveland Indians' logo from all city-owned property." (It should be noted that a city spokesman could not say whether Chief Wahoo appeared "on city buildings other than Cleveland Browns Stadium," where it flashed occasionally on message boards owned by the Browns.)

In 2014, the editorial board of the *Plain Dealer*—the newspaper that had run countless sketches of Chief Wahoo and had frequently referred to "wigwams" and "papooses" in baseball stories—called for the logo to go. The courts never succeeded in having the team remove the logo. But Major League Baseball did. In January 2018, after meeting with team officials, Commissioner Rob Manfred's desire was clear: No more Wahoo.

On October 8, 2018, the Indians hosted the Astros in Game 3 of the American League Division Series. With two outs and no one on base in the ninth inning, Cleveland's Melky Cabrera came to the plate. He hit a ground ball down the first-base line to Yuli Gurriel, who tossed it to pitcher Will Harris for the third out. Cabrera trotted off the field, the final moment fans would see Wahoo on players' uniforms. The Indians lost, 11–3. Their postseason was over, and so was Chief Wahoo.

Walter Goldbach wasn't around to see the game. He died on December 13, 2017. The family company he worked for, J.F. Novak, still exists, sitting in a nondescript building on Meyer Avenue on Cleveland's West Side. Ironically, the building where Goldbach sketched his creations is about a dozen blocks from the home on Carlyle Avenue where newspaper artist Fred Reinert lived. It's worth noting that the logo is not entirely dead. The team maintains the trademark. And nostalgia rules, especially among Cleveland fans. Routinely, eBay listings total thousands of items covering variations of Chief Wahoo. Mike Veeck, the son of maverick team owner Bill Veeck, who hired Novak/Goldbach, told ESPN's *Outside the Lines* that his father would have approved of Chief Wahoo's removal. (Mike Veeck remains as much a forward-thinking marketing and public-relations wizard in baseball as his father was.)

"Bill Veeck would've been all for the change and would've done it before now.…I think he'd be pragmatic. It was right for his team when we all watched 'cowboys and Indians.' And later, it was inappropriate. He wasn't above offending, but never deliberately hurtful. So, if it hurt people, he would've changed it right away."

Wahoo was spared in at least one way. When Cleveland Municipal Stadium was demolished, a twenty-eight-foot-high lighted logo was salvaged. It had smiled upon countless fans walking through Gate D since 1962 and was donated to Western Reserve Historical Society in 1994. But Chief Wahoo had stood in a left-handed batting stance for more than three decades and was in need of repairs. Donations rolled in, and the fact that Brilliant Sign Company of Cleveland, which has been around since 1929, still had the original plans for the mounted logo helped as well. The restored logo rests comfortably, Wahoo smiling in his batter's stance, at Western Reserve Historical Society.

As the 2021 season was about to start, the Indians announced several new policy changes, including banning fans from wearing headdresses or war paint on their faces. But the Chief Wahoo logo on apparel was still allowed.

Left: Chief Wahoo, which once welcomed fans at Cleveland Municipal Stadium, can be found in Western Reserve Historical Society's Cleveland History Center. *Chuck Crow, the Plain Dealer*.

Below: Chief Wahoo was ubiquitous on clothing, posters and logos for years. Fan Jim Stamper holds his famous Chief Wahoo sign at Progressive Field in 2017. *Marc Bona, cleveland.com*.

It's hard to envision a day when Wahoo's smiling face is not seen on shirts, caps and hoodies in a baseball stadium in Cleveland. A cleveland. com poll posted in 2019 asked fans, "Should the Cleveland Indians bring back Chief Wahoo?" More than 82 percent said yes.

5

THE TEAM THAT NEVER
HAD A CHANCE

With no debate from serious baseball fans, the 1899 Cleveland Spiders hold the dishonor of being the worst team ever. They finished the year 20-134. But why were they so bad, and who were these players?

Despite coming off an 81-68 campaign in 1898, the Spiders never had a chance. Their abysmal season was rooted in the greed of the Pittsburgh-born team owner, Frank Robison. The game and its nascent leagues were undergoing growing pains and financial challenges. Two years earlier, it was rumored that Robison was looking to move the team to Cincinnati. Discussions followed of a prospective merger with Brooklyn. Then, in 1898, Robison set his sights on buying a team in St. Louis, where he saw a potentially more lucrative fan base. (In those days, one person was allowed to own multiple teams, which seems unimaginable for any major sport today.) What Robison did is well noted in baseball history: He bought the St. Louis team and sent his best players there, including Cy Young. He left the dregs in Cleveland, had no love for the hometown fans and made it clear he didn't care.

When his manager in Cleveland asked for several solid players to field a competitive team, Robison was dismissive: "I'm not interested in winning games here," he snapped. "Play out the schedule. That's your job."

They did play out the schedule—just barely. If the standings were a building, the Spiders would have been below the foundation.

Collectively, here's what they accomplished:

The season began at St. Louis as the Spiders went down, 10–1, before eighteen thousand fans, believed to be the largest crowd to see a ballgame at Sportsman's Park at the time. It was a harbinger for Cleveland's season.

They won back-to-back games only once. Their longest losing streak stretched over twenty-four games—still a National League record. They lost forty of their final forty-one games and finished eighty-four games behind league-leading Brooklyn. (Compare the 1899 Spiders to the 2016 World Series–bound Indians, who never lost more than three in a row.)

The Spiders finished the year with a "winning" percentage of .130. Their most successful month was May, when they went 7-19. Of the twenty wins, eight were by one run.

On August 24, Cleveland hosted the New York Giants, losing 6–2; only one hundred fans showed. A day later, the Spiders beat the Giants, 4–2. After that, they won only once, a 5–4 victory in the opener of a doubleheader at Washington on September 18.

So named reportedly because of the players' skinny look, the Spiders just weren't doing anything to put fannies in the seats. At one point, gate receipts dipped below twenty-five dollars. That forced opponents to refuse to return to Cleveland. When Robison announced that virtually all of the Spiders' remaining games were shifted to visiting parks, the writers dubbed the team the "Exiles," one of many unofficial nicknames used that season. So the Spiders' last thirty-six consecutive games from August 31 to October 15 were on the road, with the team traveling the rails between St. Louis and the Atlantic Seaboard. The Spiders won a total of nine games at home and eleven on the road. And to no one's surprise, the team was dead last in attendance.

The 1899 Spiders were made up of misfits, a colorful collection of characters that left marks—mostly eclectic—on the sport through a bizarre litany of milestones.

One player died a strange death. One invented a game. Another parlayed selling cigars into playing for the team. Another was an ornery record-holder. One is credited with inventing a key piece of equipment still used in today's game.

With the Cleveland baseball headquarters basically "abandoned," as one newspaper story of the day put it, the players formed a ragtag bunch who dragged themselves out for thrashings over 154 games.

The pitching staff included Frank Bates, who, after going 2-1 in his rookie year in 1898, finished 1-18 in 1899. Harry Colliflower showed promise by winning his first game of the year on July 21. It was a trial run of sorts, and Robison liked him enough to sign him.

Colliflower finished the year 1-11.

Jim Hughey lost thirty games in 1899. He is the last major-league pitcher to lose that many games in a season. On the plus side, he had a 5.41 ERA, lowest among regular pitchers on the team.

Charlie Knepper tied Hughey with four wins apiece. Harry Maupin, who had gone 0-2 the previous season for St. Louis, went 0-3 for Cleveland. He played minor-league ball the next season, leaving behind his 0-5 two-year Major League Baseball career.

Jack Stivetts had won more than two hundred games by the time he got to the Spiders in 1899. He appeared in seven games, went 0-4 and hung up his spikes.

Then there was Crazy Schmit, who went 2-17 but not for lack of effort. He had a tendency to become wild the angrier he became on the mound. Schmit is believed to be the first pitcher to keep a book on opposing hitters. His tactics were a bit cruder than the analytical approach employed today, when statistics are computed and coaches gather with pitchers before games to go over opposing hitters. Schmit literally kept a book in his pocket and would jot notations about a hitter's tendencies.

Jack Clements, a veteran catcher who appeared in just a handful of games for the Spiders, had invented a rudimentary chest protector several years earlier. But he was cut a few games into the season after he refused to accept a pay cut to $1,500. One paper stated rather bluntly: "It is reported that old Jack Clements has been released by Cleveland. It is well known that the old boy has become too fat and did not train down a pound this spring."

Players went by names like "Buttermilk" Tommy Dowd, whose .278 was the team's second-highest average among starters, and "Highball" Wilson, who was one of fifteen pitchers to appear for the Spiders that season.

They were colorful, if not all were likeable.

Thirty-five-year-old first baseman Tommy Tucker hit .241 in what would be his final season. He was a far cry from his decade-earlier performance in 1889 when he hit .372, still a record for a switch-hitter. But by all accounts Tucker was an ornery cuss. His Society for Baseball Research biography notes, "By the time he took his last throw at first base in a major league game in 1899, few indeed were sorry to see him go." (He was hit by pitches 272 times in his career, probably at least partially due to his disposition.) In 1893, when he was with Boston, Tucker purposefully blocked Chief Zimmer off a base so forcefully that the Cleveland player broke his collarbone.

Six years later, the two were teammates on the Spiders, which would have made for interesting dugout conversation.

Zimmer—who once caught a Cy Young no-hitter—used a piece of beefsteak as padding in his crude catcher's mitt. At thirty-eight, he was the oldest player on the team.

Zimmer holds an off-the-field accomplishment as an inventor: In 1893—before the injury caused by Tucker—he created and patented a board game called "Zimmer's Base Ball Game." Only ten copies are known to exist. Late in his career the non-stogie-smoking Zimmer opened a popular cigar store. (Several years later, Ossee Schrecongost, a catcher who hit .313 in forty-three games for the 1899 Spiders, also sold cigars in the offseason.) Zimmer was the first president of the Players Protective Association, an early attempt at a union.

Zimmer, who played professionally until he was forty-six in 1907, lived to be eighty-eight and died in 1949 in Cleveland.

Chief Zimmer, who played for the 1899 Spiders, used to insert beefsteak as padding in his glove. *Benjamin K. Edwards Collection via Library of Congress.*

The task of managing this bunch initially fell to Lave Cross. Like Zimmer, he had played professionally until he was forty-six, in 1912. He was the first of four players to hit for the cycle in 1894.

While player-manager Cross was leading the Spiders to an 8-30 record, he was doing better at the plate, hitting .286. In what appears to be a promotion from Class AAA to the majors, he was shipped to St. Louis. Joe Quinn took over as Spider player-manager. He is the first Australian to make it to the majors and the only Australian-born person to manage in the big leagues to date.

Some careers were fleeting. Outfielder George Bristow signed with the Spiders in April. He was touted in the press as "a rattling good infielder and is especially strong at short stop." It wouldn't be the first time a player didn't live up to hype. Unlike the longevity of Cross (twenty-one major-league seasons) and Quinn (seventeen), by early May, he was done, his Major League Baseball career consisting of one hit in eight at-bats in three games.

Louis Sockalexis, a Penobscot Indian from Maine, had caught Robison's eye in 1897. That year, Sockalexis took the Spiders by storm. The outfielder became the paradoxical fan favorite, liked yet also the target of stereotypical cheering as war cries bellowed from the stands. In May, Robison beamed about Sockalexis, who had exceeded his expectations. He batted .338. But his affinity for alcohol and a sprained ankle suffered while he was drunk led to his average plummeting and the papers, once gushing over his prowess on the field, changing their tune. In July 1897, after the Spiders lost to Boston, a headline read, "A Wooden Indian: Sockalexis Played Very Much Like One for Once." The 1899 season, his third, would be his final one. He appeared in seven games. His footnote in history is tied to the legend that the Cleveland Indians were named after him in 1915, two years after his death at age forty-two.

While Louis Sockalexis's career accomplishments amount to promises unfulfilled, no one on the Spiders had a more fleeting major-league career than Eddie Kolb.

Kolb was a nineteen-year-old baseball-loving cigar clerk at Cincinnati's famed Gibson House. Several teams, including the Spiders, stayed at the hotel on road trips. Kolb implored Quinn to let him pitch the final game of the season. In what likely was a result of exasperation—or maybe a bribe of a box of cigars, as one writer suggests—the manager allowed the youngster to suit up. He received, as coverage the following day succinctly summarizes, a "severe drubbing." The account of the season's final games carried this stacked headline:

> *The Curtain Rung Down*
> *National League Season of 1899 Comes to an End at Last*
> *For the Finishing Touch the Forsakens Lose Two Games*
> *Players Will Arrive "Home" Today*

The "home" in quotations probably is a copy editor's semi-subtle jab at the road-slogged team that, in essence, really didn't have much of a home.

Kolb had talked his way onto the mound and gave up nineteen runs, nine of which were earned. He struck out one, yielded eighteen hits and gave up five walks. The team capped the season by recording six errors in the game. Kolb, however, did go 1-4 at the plate. It would be Kolb's first and last appearance as a major-league ballplayer, though he did play professionally for years afterward.

Infielder Charlie Ziegler had a brief career as well as a short life. Ziegler, who was born in and died in Canton, played in five games total, two of which were in 1899. Ziegler, who held a law degree from Ohio State, amounted to a late-season call-up for what appears to be a chance for regulars to rest. He played three games for Philadelphia in 1900 and then, tragically, four years later, died at age twenty-nine. He reportedly had eaten tainted food and contracted typhoid fever.

Jim Duncan suffered the strangest death of anyone on the 1899 Spiders. In 1901, he and two pals were spearfishing on the Allegheny River when they went missing. The bodies of his friends were found days later, but Duncan's remained missing. Relatives offered a $100 reward. About a week after the incident, his body turned up and officials surmised what had happened. The trio had been dynamiting fish when the concussion drowned them. A stick of dynamite with fuse was found in a pocket of one of the men.

In 1899, Bill Hill won 7 games for three teams, including the basement-dwelling Spiders and the league-leading Brooklyn Superbas, who won 101 games.

For the record, St. Louis—which Robison had stockpiled with Cleveland's former great players—finished in fifth place. The Robisons (Frank's brother Stanley was a part-owner) sold the Spiders' assets to Charles Somers and John Kilfoyle in 1900. The new owners kept the team afloat as a minor-league franchise called the Cleveland Lake Shores in the Western League. The Lake Shores shuttled names and leagues and eventually became the Cleveland Naps.

Throughout his years as the owner of the St. Louis baseball club, Frank Robison continued to maintain his Ohio residence. Robison's main business was rail lines that ran out to League Park.

The Robisons did have one positive residual effect on baseball. When Stanley died in 1911, three years after Frank, the only remaining heirs were women. Frank's daughter, Helene, became the first female owner in the major leagues when she inherited the St. Louis ball club. She persevered through her willingness and determination to stand up to an old-boys' club as she mustered through a divorce, contracts and other challenges.

Despite much of their success coming outside of Ohio, Frank, Stanley and Helene are all buried in Cleveland's Lake View Cemetery.

6

On a Crusade

In 1976, the Cleveland Crusaders finished their fourth and final unremarkable season in the World Hockey Association (WHA). But they made up for an uneventful line in the record books with a colorful collection of incidents and players.

They had not one but two players whose religious beliefs would alter their lives. One of the game's greatest goalies spent four years of his long career in Cleveland. One of the wackiest All-Star Game formats ever used in any sport was featured for one year—in Cleveland. It was a turbulent time that saw players revolt against their own team management.

It all started with a promise.

Nick Mileti, original owner of the Crusaders, announced the name of the team on July 6, 1972. "The new name speaks well for the excitement of the new team and the new league," he said.

What followed were four lackluster years on the ice and in the stands. The team's history did include a players' revolt against owners, which made for great fodder in the papers.

A quick account of recent Cleveland hockey history: The original Cleveland Barons played in the American Hockey League for more than thirty years until Mileti moved them to Jacksonville for the 1973–74 season, leaving the city open for a major-league team. The WHA—a rival upstart to the more established National Hockey League—awarded a franchise to Cleveland in June 1972. Mileti didn't finish out the team's four-year existence; he sold the Crusaders to Jay Moore in March 1975.

Cleveland Crusaders owner Nick Mileti. *Richard J. Misch, the Plain Dealer.*

Six players wore the Crusader uniform for at least parts of all four seasons—Gerry Cheevers, Gary Jarrett, Wayne Muloin, Gerry Pinder, Paul Shmyr and Bob Whidden. Cheevers is the only Hall of Famer from the team. He and Shmyr are also in the WHA Hall of Fame.

Often called the "C's" in newspaper stories, the Crusaders skated first in the Cleveland Arena and then the Richfield Coliseum. The team wore jerseys

An arrow denotes Paul Shmyr on this Cleveland Crusaders team photo. To his right is goaltending great Gerry Cheevers. Above, to Shmyr's right shoulder, is Tom Edur. *Author collection.*

adorned with the silhouette of a Crusader on horseback with a variation of a Jerusalem cross on his shield. At one point, a bumper sticker touted the team with the slogan "Spear 'um Crusaders," showing a horse-riding jouster with a puck at the end of his spear near a net. Obviously, the sticker's maker was not a hockey fan; spearing remains a potential injury-causing infraction and draws a major penalty.

There were some positive moments in 1976, the team's final season. Shmyr edged forward Jim Harrison—"a joy to watch this season"—as Most Valuable Crusader. Shmyr received $4,000 for being named the league's top defenseman.

Behind the scenes, though, financial and other challenges tore at the league and team. Despite higher salaries offered as a competitive draw, "the WHA's economic environment was never secure," writes David Ward in his biography of Harrison. And Harrison bluntly describes how precarious the times were. "We always carried our skates with us," he said, "just in case our equipment was seized by the bank."

If you had to find new equipment that was one thing, but if you didn't have your own skates, you couldn't play. Seriously, it was a lot of fun and we all made good money, but you never knew if your next paycheque was going to bounce. That's why I left Cleveland—they bounced cheques on me.... They'd built their arena way out in the country and they weren't drawing any fans. We had a bunch of characters on that club, so we had a lot of fun, but the fun stops pretty quick when the cheques start bouncing.

Longtime *Plain Dealer* sportswriter Chuck Heaton described the team's final year as "a season of turbulence." Or, as beat writer Jeff Passan wrote, "The C's have accomplished the impossible by outdoing themselves for the fourth straight season in zaniness."

Passan, who wrote a regular column for years called "Passin' the Puck" and covered hockey in Cleveland from 1965 to 1977, once gave awards in print that included "Biggest bumblers—a tie between the Crusaders' front office and the World Hockey Association board of trustees. Ineptitude flowed from these two groups."

On April 6, the Crusaders lost to the San Diego Mariners, 3–2. Jay Moore's frustration over lack of calls in the game led him to douse referee Bob Kolari with beer. Fan attendance never was enough to keep the team

Cleveland Crusader owner Nick Mileti and goaltender Gerry Cheevers. *William A. Ashbolt, the Plain Dealer.*

in the black. After the team's final season, one hockey official categorized the fans' experience in Cleveland with the Crusaders as "acrid," saying, "There was friction between fans, players and press last season." The lackluster turnout was partly because the Cavaliers owned choice weekend calendar dates and partly because the Crusaders were a non-major-league franchise playing in a major-league town. Cheevers had enough and bolted during the team's final season for his old team, the Boston Bruins. Jack Vivian, the Crusaders' general manager, resigned four times in his two-year stint with the team. Two of those times actually came in the same month.

Then came the infamous black-armband game. On March 10, 1976, the

Crusaders were set to host the Cincinnati Stingers. The team had voted to wear the mourning bands as a sign of protest against Moore's efforts to bring in the NHL's Kansas City Scouts to Cleveland. That is akin to your parents adopting someone and forgetting about their natural-born children. "We've got to do something for the fans' benefit and our own self pride….All the guys are ticked off and I can't blame them," said Shmyr, team captain. Moore tried to talk them out of it, but the game went on with the Crusaders wearing the bands on their left arms. (The bands were a short-term salve for the Crusaders, who beat the Stingers, 5–2, before a crowd of 12,286 at the Coliseum. The higher-than-average attendance figure was due more to a Geauga Lake Amusement Park promotion rather than Clevelanders turning out to support the home team in their opposition to management.)

Ironically, Cleveland hosted the WHA All-Star Game in what turned out to be the Crusaders' final season. When a city hosts an All-Star Game, it gets a chance to shine, to put on its Sunday best and strut a bit. Major League Baseball, for instance, has evolved its game into an entertainment showcase that goes on for days, as seen with the 2019 Midsummer Classic in Cleveland. But that didn't happen in 1976.

Like a person trying on clothes to find the right fit and style, the league bounced around formats of the game. In all, nine games were played in varying formats over the league's seven-year existence. On January 13, 1976, the game took on a unique shape: Canada versus United States. But the teams were not based on players' nationality but rather on franchise locations. So a Canadian-born player on a team in the United States would play for the U.S. squad while an American native playing for one of the teams up North would compete for Canada. For this, fans paid $6.50 for an upper-mezzanine seat at the Coliseum. Canada won, 6–1. A third-period goal from Andre Lacroix before 15,491 fans—a WHA-All-Star Game attendance record—saved the "Americans" from a shutout. Teenager Real Cloutier (Canada) and Shmyr (United States) were named MVPs. Each received a car. Cloutier, through an interpreter, said he did not even know what kind of car he won, though it was his third one.

The most amazing thing about the game might have been that Toronto's Joe Shaw was a last-minute sub in goal for Canada. He had been planning on staying home to watch the game over a few beers when he was notified he was needed to get to Cleveland to fill in for an ill goaltender. The All-Star team practiced at 3:30 p.m., and he caught a 5:00 p.m. flight. Shaw, with a 4.90 goals-against average, made it by 7:45 p.m. Faceoff was scheduled for 8:00 p.m.

The promotional aspect of the game was nonexistent. No All-Star items were sold at the arena, only Crusaders and Cavaliers gear. There were no special painted emblems embedded on the ice, and the start of the game was delayed for ice resurfacing. But fans were able to see two of the sport's greatest players, right-wing Gordie Howe and left-wing Bobby Hull, face each other. It also marked the first time that members of hockey's first family—the Howes—appeared together in an All-Star Game, as dad Gordie and sons Mark and Marty suited up.

Two of Cleveland's players, Tom Edur and John Stewart, were atypical athletes of their day. Edur was eighteen when he signed a three-year contract worth $175,000 with Cleveland, making him the youngest player in the WHA. He was coming off a season when he had fourteen goals and forty-eight assists for sixty-two points in fifty-seven games for Toronto in the Ontario Hockey Association. His signing promoted controversy and added to the acrimonious relationship between the WHA and the NHL. The National Hockey League had a deal with the Canadian Amateur Hockey Association, preventing the NHL from selecting players before their junior eligibility was up. Edur's WHA signing rankled the NHL enough to consider changing its agreement.

Edur came onto the scene as a "baby-faced blond" and proceeded to play with the Crusaders for the team's final three years. He then played two years with Colorado in the NHL before moving to the Pittsburgh Penguins for the 1977–78 season. A productive defenseman, he drew praise in game accounts, a promising career taking off. And then, all of a sudden, at age twenty-three, he retired.

Edur walked away from his $92,000 annual salary and the league he had dreamed of playing in since he was ten. "I quit hockey, but not because I don't love the game. I do. My dream had been to become a National Hockey League player....I would play after school and late into the night—until the lights at the ice rink were finally turned off."

Years later, he discussed his career and reason for quitting. The Crusaders had offered him $250,000 for three years, a heady offer for a teenager. But the sheen of stardom that comes with realizing what a professional hockey player was about, Edur said, wore off quickly. Hockey, he learned, wasn't so much about what was on the ice but off. It was about drinking and carousing, as he saw it. Over time, he saw his play deteriorate, but he still saw what he viewed as "drunkenness and immorality" around him. A trip home for his grandmother's funeral in 1977 led him to seriously question his life, that self-awareness that comes only when we truly examine ourselves. He became reacquainted with a friend from high school who had just started to study with Jehovah's Witnesses. He began reading, and an introspective summer led him to the belief that the religion should be his calling.

"I reached the conclusion that Bible principles and professional hockey just don't mix." At one point, he elaborated, saying, "My faith is a way of life, and there are things in hockey, like the violence and killer instinct, which don't coincide with the Bible's principles." He played for Pittsburgh while mulling his decision. His gut and his heart told him to give up the sport, and in September 1978, he informed the team he was done.

Initially, the Penguins tried to persuade him to reconsider. They said he could have Sundays off. Then they offered him $20,000 to play two weekend games. But he was finished.

"I don't like to do anything halfway," he said. "I came to the conclusion it had to be one way or the other." He said his life would be based on "door-to-door preaching." "I want to do things that are pleasing to Jehovah, and I feel hockey is not one of those things. When I play hockey I want to play 100 percent, and I don't want anything interfering with that. I can't split my devotion."

Some sneered at Edur's decision. When asked which principles of faith would prevent Edur from playing hockey, Pittsburgh general manager Baz Bastien guessed "thou shalt not brawl." A headline in one paper's announcement of Edur's retirement read "Edur Turns Other Cheek." David Rubinstein, the Penguins' marketing director, joked that the team received something in return for Edur's retirement. "We got compensation from God," he said, "Two miracles."

Edur was as consistent and focused in his decision as a player on a breakaway. In 1990, he moved to Estonia as part of his religious work. Jay Noble, an autograph seeker in Canada, said Edur "never looked back and in his letter back to me wrote that he never regretted the decision."

In a 1993 story about religious freedom in Russia, Edur was quoted, saying he hoped for freedom, as laws threatened missionary work. In 2014, he underwent surgery to remove a brain tumor, one he surmises came from the hits he took on the ice, he told Noble.

John Stewart, one of Edur's teammates during the Crusaders' final year, would take a similar path in life. (The Crusaders actually had two John Stewarts playing together in the final season. Both were six-foot, 180-pound players. Passan said, "Both were quiet, do-your-job kind of guys." He added: "When both played in the same game and factored in the game story, it required a strict mindset to make certain I got the correct middle initial.")

In the Crusaders' final season, John A. Stewart accounted for twelve goals and twenty-one assists for thirty-three points in seventy-nine games.

About halfway through his hockey career, he was invited to attend church services. Stewart's move into religion wasn't as epiphanic as Edur's but was just as strong. After his career, Stewart graduated from Central Baptist Theological Seminary. He worked as a pastor dedicated to discipleship but developed a niche writing Bible-study guides. That led him to found Lamplighters International in 2000.

His career choice surprised even him, he once told a reporter. "If somebody had given me a list of 1,000 possible careers I could pursue after hockey, I would have ranked 'minister' and 'writer' as the last two," he said. "I had barely managed to finish high school, I hadn't read anything other than *Sports Illustrated* and I had a vocabulary that consisted of 12 words, all of them profane."

As of this writing, Stewart and Edur are both continuing in their respective religious work. Neither was the first sports figure to go into evangelizing. Nineteenth-century baseball star Billy Sunday holds that distinction. But two players on the same team, and named Crusaders?

The Crusaders averaged about 6,200 fans and won only one playoff series in four years, never winning their division. They had two seasons above .500.

Attendance was a key factor in the team not returning. Moore once said that the team needed eight thousand fans to meet payroll and twelve thousand to break even. In April 1976, though, he told a reporter that the city would have a WHA team the following season. But a month later, Passan reported that the team's chances of returning were 50-50. In fifteen months, Moore, it was reported, had dumped more than $1 million into the franchise. Weeks later, he was entertaining the sale of the team to Bill Putnam, who planned to move it to Hollywood, Florida. The Crusaders had hit a fork in the road, in an odd way. They would go to Florida under Putnam's new ownership or they would head to Minnesota as the Fighting Saints, with Mileti back running things. Either way, it seemed Cleveland would be left without a professional hockey team.

The Florida deal, worth $1.4 million, never materialized. The team headed north to play in St. Paul as the Minnesota Fighting Saints. They didn't last a season.

Cheevers didn't finish out that final season with the Crusaders, choosing to return to the Boston Bruins, where he spent the last five years of his career, retiring in 1980 and going down as one the game's greatest goalies. Shmyr remained in the WHA for three more seasons and then returned to the NHL. He spent seven seasons in each league before retiring after the 1981–82 season.

If you're an NHL fan in the NHL-team-less city of Cleveland and you like history, you might want to cheer for the Dallas Stars. Follow this: After the demise of the Crusaders, the NHL's California Golden Seals were moved to Cleveland and became the second version of the Barons for two seasons (1976–78). The Barons then were merged into the Minnesota North Stars, which, in 1993, moved south to become the Dallas Stars.

One final footnote: There is an ignoble connection with Cleveland, hockey and tragedy in the world of sports. In 1920, Cleveland Indian Ray Chapman was the only major-league player to die from injuries from being struck by a pitched ball. In 1968, a helmet-less Bill Masterton of the Minnesota North Stars was killed when he hit his head on the ice. In 1962–63, he had played his sole season in the American Hockey League, arguably his best season as a professional. The AHL team he played for? The Cleveland Barons.

7

BOSS MEN

The Steinbrenner-Owned Indians and the Strongsville Browns

One well-known owner in professional sports history got his start in Cleveland and moved on to New York. Another began his career in New York before landing in Cleveland. Both share a couple of traits, including the ignoble status of being two of the most hated owners in sports history. Their stories are interesting, but their impact on Cleveland becomes an intriguing string of potential what-if scenarios. They are George Steinbrenner and Art Modell.

What they did in their careers is well known: Steinbrenner became the dictatorial boss of Yankee Stadium, while Modell would be remembered for moving the Cleveland Browns out of the city in the 1990s. But the intrigue lies in the deals they came close to making in Cleveland.

Their stories really start in the 1960s. In 1962, frozen-foods magnate and Cleveland native Vernon Stouffer became a Tribe stockholder. Four years later, it was announced that he would buy the team. In 1964, CBS purchased the Yankees. Both owners would regret their decisions.

Stouffer bought 80 percent of the team for $8 million. The Indians under his ownership finished above .500 only twice and never higher than third place. He would own the team until 1972.

Meanwhile, as the team was floundering, a group of well-heeled businessmen including Steinbrenner met regularly at the Pewter Club in downtown Cleveland, holding court at a regular table. Among his fellow sports fans, the Ohio native Steinbrenner admitted that he always wanted to buy the Indians.

In 1971, Stouffer was mulling the idea of the team playing games in New Orleans, a city that was making overtures to buy and move the Indians out of the forty-plus-year-old Municipal Stadium.

New Orleans offered a real possibility to lure the team for a share of games to be played in the soon-to-be-built Superdome. One of the deal's attractive draws for the Indians was being able to cut into two media markets for its fan base. Cleveland mayor Ralph Perk had tied needed improvements in Municipal Stadium to the team agreeing to a long-term lease.

Like a captain peering from a ship's bow, Steinbrenner kept tabs on the Indians and their future. At this point, Steinbrenner had no vested interest in team ownership. His main business was the family shipbuilding company.

Ironically, baseball wasn't the sport he was into at a young age. Steinbrenner was born in Rocky River and ran track. He put off the family business as long as he could, receiving a master's degree at Ohio State and coaching football at the Division I level. He eventually cut his teeth on professional sports-team ownership when he bought the Cleveland Pipers basketball team in 1961.

While he was recognized behind the scenes as a philanthropist, publicly, Steinbrenner was known for his "mercurial tendencies," noted Vince Guerrieri, his Society for American Baseball Research biographer.

Regardless of opinions that formed around Steinbrenner, during his time in Cleveland, he was viewed as "one of the city's captains of industry."

Sheldon Guren, the president of U.S. Realty, was one of the power-lunch brokers in Steinbrenner's circle of pals. Guren assembled a meeting that included Steinbrenner and Modell. Modell had owned the Browns since 1961. The rumor was that developer Edward DeBartolo was interested in building two stadiums south of Cleveland for racetracks as well as football and baseball. The vision was a simple one: Modell could move the Browns, and Al Rosen—former Tribe great turned stockbroker—could put together investors for the Indians. Rosen immediately contacted Steinbrenner.

"This has been my dream," Steinbrenner said.

Despite the initial conversation turning into several meetings, that out-of-Cleveland stadium concept never materialized. But talks between Stouffer and Steinbrenner did.

In 1971, Stouffer wanted $9 million for the Indians; Steinbrenner was looking to pay $6 million. (Stouffer had paid about $8 million for the team.)

Steinbrenner and Stouffer's son Jimmy were friends; they had attended Culver Military Academy together. The two men agreed on an $8.6 million deal. The only thing that remained was Vernon Stouffer signing off.

New York Yankee owner George Steinbrenner attends the Indians' home opener on April 13, 1985. More than a decade earlier, Steinbrenner came extremely close to buying the Indians. *Jim Gayle, the Plain Dealer.*

Steinbrenner and Rosen waited in Steinbrenner's downtown Cleveland office. The deal wasn't signed, but it appeared done—enough so that Marsh Samuel began writing a press release to announce the sale of the team to Steinbrenner. Samuel had been the Indians' public-relations chief from 1947 to 1952 and was a pioneer in creating an extensive media guide. Suffice to say, that release would have had a chance to wind up in the Baseball Hall of Fame in Cooperstown, New York.

Reporters were called and assembled at the office. Steinbrenner sat by the phone and waited for the call from Stouffer, who was in Arizona. A little after 5:00 p.m., the phone rang. But instead of Stouffer crossing the t's and dotting the i's on the deal, he had come down with a case of cold feet, fueled by a drink or two. "I'm not doing this deal," Stouffer said. The announcement that would have altered baseball history never came. Reporters left.

Steinbrenner's disappointment would wane the following summer, when he learned that the Yankees were for sale. Like Stouffer being unhappy with the way things were going for his team, CBS—the Yankees' owner—had had enough. The Yankees had lost the 1964 World Series and then didn't make the postseason for more than a decade. CBS wanted out. Within

Art Modell bought the Cleveland Browns in 1961. *Dudley Brumbach, the Plain Dealer.*

months, the deal was completed for $10 million (though a buyback provision for city garages in the arrangement put the real price around $8.8 million). CBS had paid $16 million for the team fewer than ten years earlier.

According to longtime *New York Daily News* baseball writer Bill Madden in his 2010 book *George Steinbrenner: The Last Lion of Baseball*, Steinbrenner uttered a comment to CBS chairman Bill Paley regarding the transition of the team's ownership. It would ring as an infamous falsehood. "I've got a ship company to run. I won't have much time for baseball."

Modell's story also involves a deal and parallels to Steinbrenner's.

Modell paid $4 million for the Browns in 1961. He had started out working in the nascent days of television advertising. The pinnacle of his sports ownership came three years later, when the Browns won the 1964 championship against Baltimore.

Like Steinbrenner, who had ventured into basketball in the 1960s, Modell kept his eye on that sport as well. He was responsible for a deal that saw the Cincinnati Royals play games in Cleveland in 1967.

In 1972 and 1973, Modell bought about 192 acres in Strongsville. (The exact number was listed as different amounts over time, but the 192 figure appeared in court papers regarding a messy lawsuit brought by Bob Gries, who owned a share of the Browns.)

The land deal was a prudent move; a study showed that a majority of Brown fans lived in the suburbs of Cleveland.

"My only interest there (Strongsville) is as a fallback in case nothing is started to improve the Stadium in the next two years. I don't want to see further decay of the stadium," Modell said.

Modell had gone after once-rural land in Strongsville about twenty miles southwest of downtown Cleveland. He bought seven individually owned parcels and was considering building an eighty-thousand-seat stadium on fewer than ten of those acres. Bishop Realty brokered the deal. (In 1973, one of Bishop Realty's employees was Mike Phipps, though the Browns quarterback—in his off-season gig—was not involved in that particular transaction).

The location Modell was considering included land just southwest of Ohio 82 and Interstate 71. The land eventually became one of several focal points in Gries's lawsuit, which challenged Modell's financial stake in Cleveland Stadium Corp. According to a report done for Modell, the land was valued at $3.8 million. Among other claims, Gries said that was ten times too much.

One story characterized the land as "gently rolling, virtually clear, former farmland" but said local zoning approval still would be needed, despite the potential financial boon for Strongsville.

In 1973, Strongsville City Council was divided on the idea of a stadium being developed.

The question remains as to how much of Modell's posturing to move the team was rooted in reality as opposed to his position masquerading as a threat because Cleveland Municipal Stadium needed refurbishing. In 1973, the Indians and the Browns signed a one-year deal to lease the stadium.

In the end, Modell signed a twenty-five-year lease, and the Browns stayed put.

(Vernon Stouffer, in a way, was tied to both men. In addition to the Strongsville land deal that did not develop into a stadium, Modell owned a stake in Stouffer's Inn on the Square, which later became Renaissance Cleveland Hotel. He also held a nonvoting seat on the Indians' board of directors.)

The what-if scenarios also add up to an interesting point that would have changed the face of downtown for decades. In 1974, the Cavaliers left Cleveland for Richfield in Summit County. If the Indians had moved—a possibility being tossed about then—and the Browns were to follow the suburban route the Cavs took, Cleveland would have been left without a major sports franchise. What this would have meant for the massive Depression-era Cleveland Municipal Stadium is, of course, unknown. Would it have hastened the Indians or the city to build a baseball-only park prior to 1994? And, if it were to be demolished, the shape of downtown would look considerably different today. What would have happened to the Gateway area, where Progressive Field is located? And would Strongsville have included an area similar to the well-known muni lot for Browns fans to dress up, drive in and tailgate?

But the true collection of what-if questions that will keep Indian fans in particular up at night begins with this one: How would the team have done had Steinbrenner owned them instead of the Yankees?

Would his willingness to whip out the checkbook have brought high-profile players to the Indians? Cleveland was in the American League East from

1969 through 1993. In that time, they finished above .500 four times. It was Steinbrenner's magnanimous financial approach that had a huge impact on the sport as well as on the Yankees. In the 1970s, million-dollar contracts were big news. He signed Catfish Hunter to a $3.75 million contract. In the early years of free agency, Steinbrenner signed ten players for about $38 million. He inked slugger Dave Winfield to an $18.2 million, ten-year contract, viewed as the richest free-agent signing ever. Would signings of those or similar players have lifted the Tribe into a contending team in those lean years?

On the negative side, it's worth considering whether there would have been a revolving door for Tribe managers like the one in Yankee Stadium. Yankee skippers were as changeable during Steinbrenner's tenure as Browns starting quarterbacks in recent memory. And it's a safe bet that Steinbrenner's proclivity to enforce a facial-hair policy regarding his players would have been applied in Cleveland.

THE AFTERMATH

In 1972, Stouffer sold the team to Nick Mileti, who paid closer to the asking price. At the time, New Orleans was making a bid for the Indians, but Mileti kept them where they were.

The year 1973 turned out to be a big one for all players involved, including the city of Cleveland. Steinbrenner had inked the deal for the Yankees, and Modell was buying the land in Strongsville. But the new Yankee boss also was trying to buy something else: favors. He was one of several people at his shipbuilding company tied to illegal donations to the Committee to Re-elect the President. The following year, he pled guilty to felony and misdemeanor charges regarding the donations. (In 1974, Stouffer died. He, too, was a big donor to President Richard Nixon and had given $15,000 to the colorfully known "CREEP" coffers.)

In 1975, Modell sold the Strongsville land to Cleveland Stadium Corp., which he had helped form two years prior. He sold the land to CSC for $4 million. Just a few years earlier, he had bought the land for $800,000.

Rosen went to New York in the late 1970s as president of the Yankees. Modell's Strongsville land eventually was developed as SouthPark Mall, which opened in 1996.

Steinbrenner officially left Northeast Ohio in 1983, when AmShip (American Ship Building Company) closed its operations in Lorain and headed south to Tampa. The Florida city eventually became the Yankees' spring-training site.

The Yankees endured lackluster seasons from 1965 to 1975 and then began rising in the standings to the consistent pennant-contending team they once were. And as the won-loss records improved, so did Steinbrenner's investment. As Guerrieri wrote in his SABR bio published in 2020: "In 2009, the team Steinbrenner bought for $10 million—with an outlay of just $168,000 of his own money—was valued at $1.5 billion. The Yankees were thus the third most valuable franchise in pro sports, trailing just English Premier League soccer team Manchester United and the Dallas Cowboys."

The free-agent signings and the team's fortunes make one Cleveland writer's comments in 1972 particularly speculative: "Now I'm wishing Steinbrenner's group had succeeded in getting the Indians. It doesn't appear Mileti's group will be able to give the Tribe the desperately needed personal attention it needs....With Steinbrenner's no-foolishness approach, the Indians might find a firm hand just the ticket."

It's probably safe to say that Cleveland would not have mellowed George Steinbrenner. But the city has not been much for mellowing and forgiveness. Clevelanders still cling to a grudge about Modell moving the Browns to Baltimore in the mid-1990s. The city was without an NFL team from the 1996 to the 1998 seasons. In those three years, the Baltimore Ravens won only sixteen games. But two years later, after the 2000 season, they won the Super Bowl.

Steinbrenner, who got his start in Cleveland, died in 2010. Modell, who came to Cleveland, died in 2012. Neither is buried here.

8

THE BIG (LINE)MAN

To excel at one thing in life is a treat. But to be great at two passions? That's a rare, heavenly gift, unthinkable for most of us. It's a blessing. And one man who came close to making Cleveland his home was so blessed.

His parents gave him a saxophone when he was nine, and a love of music was nurtured. He also was a big kid, playing defensive end at Crestwood High School in Virginia. He was good enough to play at Maryland State University among the ranks of Historically Black Colleges and Universities. He anchored the offensive line at center and end on defense. In college, he was six feet, two inches and 250 pounds—and then had a bit of a growth spurt. And he played hard. "When he brought it," a college teammate said, "he brought it every play."

He also showed improvement, enough to be touted as a potential draft pick in December 1963.

Another college teammate described him as being seriously into music, even more so than football.

In 1966, the young man left home and drove up the coast, heading for New York City, its multitude of clubs beckoning for gigs. Music was on his mind, but football wasn't forgotten.

He eventually landed a steady job, working at a reform school, helping guide and mentor kids. He also made a semipro football team, the Jersey Generals, earning about $100 a game. Coverage in that play-both-ways era viewed him as "certain" to see playing time at center and a "standout" at defensive tackle. One account said he did a "superlative job" in a 40–18 win over the Shamrocks of Marlboro, Massachusetts.

During a practice with the Generals—by all accounts a good team—he apparently caught the eye of a scout for the Cleveland Browns, who sent word that he wanted the young player to try out in Newark, New Jersey. (At some point along the way, the Dallas Cowboys also reportedly were interested.)

But the day before he was to show the Browns what he could do, the path his life was on shifted suddenly. The football/music crossroads would be reached. He wrote about the event years later.

> *All that changed in 1968 when the accelerator jammed on that dark blue Riviera on the long, tree-lined driveway, leading to the crowded square in front of the school. The car shot up to a hundred miles an hour in seconds. A motor mount had snapped, and there was no way to stop the car. I tried the emergency brake but nothing happened. Finally I took my eyes off the road and bent down to physically lift the gas pedal. It was a desperate move and it failed. When I got back up behind the wheel I was inches away from the tree.*
>
> *There was no pain. No pain at all. I was floating up above my body watching the paramedics work on me. I heard one of them say I was gone. But I was there in this light. All I felt was euphoria. I felt like I should let go, but then I thought "I'm not finished. I've got to go back." So I did.*

Among other injuries, he had nearly torn off an ear. "I was by myself, thank God," he said. The accident made his life choice for him.

He never played football again. "I was looking at a pro career," he said. "God had other plans."

The door to football had closed, leaving the one to music open for the man with dual talents.

In 1971, the young man met his college teammate at a restaurant in New York. The teammate, Emerson Boozer, had gone on to a solid career as a running back in the NFL with the New York Jets.

"I asked him what he was doing, and he told me that he had met a blue-eyed soul brother who was going to make him a lot of money," Boozer said. "I asked him what he meant, and he said that he had met a young fella who could really sing, who stirs the crowd, gets them all involved. He said write this down and don't forget it: Bruce Springsteen."

The big lineman was Clarence Clemons, longtime saxophone player for Springsteen's E Street Band. Clemons had met the budding rock star in

Clarence Clemons in college.
*University of Maryland Eastern Shore,
Princess Anne, Maryland.*

1971 and soon became more than just a horn player in a backup band. He was a sidekick, a confidant, a presence. The two played together for almost forty years, energetic show after show.

But, as Boozer said, "He was good enough to play pro, there's no question about it."

A couple of what-ifs tantalize Brown fans here. What if the accelerator doesn't jam and Clemons doesn't get into the accident but instead makes his tryout? If he impresses scouts, the money offered—whatever it might be—would have been too much for a twenty-six-year-old to turn down, along with the chance for NFL glory.

Would he have been relegated to offense as a center or defense as an end, or would he have played both?

It is also worth noting that he would have been blocking for future Hall of Famer Leroy Kelly. And what if Jim Brown hadn't retired so soon? When production of a film Brown was working on delayed him from getting to training camp on time, team owner Art Modell stubbornly dug in his heels and threatened to fine his star running back. Brown might have been piling more yards on to his total, running behind Clemons. Brown was twenty-nine and coming off a superb season when he quit. The thinking is that he could have kept going.

Bruce Springsteen performs with the E Street Band at Quicken Loans Arena in Cleveland on February 23, 2016. Clarence Clemons was a longtime sidekick to "The Boss." *Lisa DeJong, the Plain Dealer.*

Had it worked out with the Cowboys instead of the Browns, Clemons might have been hiking the ball to a young Roger Staubach, who made his professional debut in 1969 and went on to a stellar eleven-year career in Dallas.

Finally, had Clemons made it to the NFL, the effect on Springsteen without his sax man remains a guess. Much has been written on the fast friendship that developed between the two. Would Springsteen have found someone else? Would the chemistry that fans came to embrace have developed with someone else? It's hard to imagine.

"Together, we told an older, richer story about the possibilities of friendship that transcended those I'd written in my songs and in my music. Clarence carried it in his heart," Springsteen wrote in an eloquent eulogy of his friend.

Maryland State became the University of Maryland Eastern Shore in 1970. The college, located in Princess Anne, Maryland, no longer has a football team. Later in life, Clemons—a music-education major—was involved with trying to raise money to revive the program. "I really want to get football back at that school," he said, "because if not for football, I wouldn't be where I am today."

Could he have made it? Don Reo, one of his closest friends and cowriter of Clemons's book, *Big Man*, said he truly believes Clemons would have made a great football player. Clemons, Reo said, "did say that he believed in his heart that he could've made the pros. I believe it too. Once he set his mind to something it was almost like he willed it to happen."

William C. Rhoden, writing in 2011 about Clemons's death, called his legacy "rich and timeless," noting both his musical acumen and prowess on the football field.

"Either way you play it," he wrote, "that's a life well lived."

9

SOMETHING OLD, SOMETHING NEW... AND A SIXPENCE IN HER SHOE

In Cleveland, no matter how old or young, every Brown fan has heard the story of the 1964 team, the underdogs upsetting the heavily favored Baltimore Colts in Cleveland Municipal Stadium.

We won't offer a play-by-play account of the game or biographical portraits of the players, both of which have been written about repeatedly. After a recap, there are nuggets of information that might surprise even die-hard fans.

The sold-out game on December 27 packed in 79,544 fans in temperatures that hovered around freezing and saw a trace of snow. Tickets cost six, eight and ten dollars. Leading up to the game, about 2,500 standing-room tickets remained at six dollars. The game famously was blacked out on television within a seventy-five-mile radius of Cleveland. Hotel rooms were booked east and west, from Erie, Pennsylvania, to Toledo. The game was aired on radio in Cleveland on WDOK featuring local announcing veteran Ken Coleman.

By the time kickoff rolled around, it was a brisk afternoon. Bill Marting, an Akron native who was then a high school student at Western Reserve Academy in Hudson, attended the game with a pal whose father had gotten tickets. His friend's father wore "electric socks" with battery-powered heating coils. "I'd never heard of that," Marting said in recalling his experience.

But looking at the Browns, Cleveland never should have been a steep underdog. Statistically, the teams matched up fairly evenly. The Browns finished atop the East Division, and the Colts were champions of the

West in the fourteen-team league. But Baltimore had most of the stars, garnering end-of-season honors. Quarterback Johnny Unitas earned three of four Player of the Year honors; his halfback-flanker teammate Lenny Moore won the other. Don Shula—who was born in Grand River and went to high school in Painesville and college at John Carroll University in Cleveland—was named Coach of the Year. (Several Colt coaches had Cleveland ties. Offensive backfield coach Don McCafferty went to Rhodes High, played at Ohio State and coached at Kent State before his pro-coaching career. Offensive line coach John Sandusky was the Browns' second-round draft choice in 1950. He went on to play for Cleveland for six seasons. And defensive coordinator Charley Winner had been an assistant at Case Tech in the early 1950s.)

The Colts brought a league-best 12-2 record into the game, the first NFL championship to be televised by CBS. After losing their first game of the year, 34–24, at Minnesota, they reeled off eleven consecutive victories before losing again, at home to Detroit, 31–14. The Browns finished 10-3-1, including losses in two of their four final regular-season games.

Cleveland Brown players after a November 1964 game. A month later, the team would win the championship. *Robert J. Quinlan, the Plain Dealer*.

On December 15, initial odds were released favoring the Colts by five points. That line would inch up to seven by kickoff less than two weeks later.

Predictions were across the board, locally and nationally. On the day of the game, Bill Veeck, former owner of the Cleveland Indians, had written a syndicated column in which he said "the Colts will fall on the Browns like a mugger upon a drunk." Cleveland quarterback Frank Ryan made the bold and exact prediction that his team would win, 33–17. *Plain Dealer* sports columnist Chuck Heaton forecast bluntly the day of the game: "The underdog Browns will beat the Baltimore Colts this afternoon and bring the National Football League title back to Cleveland." Cleveland mayor Ralph Locher wagered maple syrup to Baltimore mayor Theodore McKeldin, who put up oysters. Locher actually gave three points in the bet. (During the mayors' terms—Locher (1962–67) and McKeldin (1963–67)—the football teams in their cities never had a losing season.) The *Plain Dealer*'s James E. Doyle, who often penned bits of verse on the sports pages, wrote this ditty:

> *Kind men who run the booking joints*
> *Will give you half a dozen points*
> *If on the Browns you'd like to bet*
> *Against that Baltimore jet set*
> *An after-Christmas bargain spot?*
> *Not quite, but still it's worth a shot*

Unitas was the Colts' gifted passer who would become one of fewer than two dozen quarterbacks to throw for forty thousand yards. He threw at least one touchdown pass every game from 1956 through 1960, a record that stood for more than half a century and is remarkable considering it came when the game was built on a more ground-based attack. The Browns countered with Frank Ryan, who trotted out an IQ of 155 and was a math professor at Case Tech in the off-season. An erudite player for his—or any—era, Ryan kept eight to ten games of chess going through the mail as a hobby. He also earned a PhD in math during his career. On paper, Unitas was the man, and he was a big reason the Colts were favored as a road team, despite the Browns having the league's rushing leader, Jim Brown.

But on December 27, 1964, it was Ryan, behind a staunch offensive line, who outshone his lauded counterpart. He was thrown for a loss only once. The teams battled through a stubborn scoreless first half, but the Browns pulled away. Ryan completed eleven of eighteen passes for 206 yards; Unitas was twelve of twenty for 95 yards. Raymond Berry, the Colts' exact route runner, was held to 38 yards on three catches.

Lou Groza kicked two field goals, and the Browns rolled to a 27–0 victory. Brown rushed twenty-seven times for 114 yards, which included a 46-yard run. Gary Collins was named the game's MVP, with five catches for 130 yards and three touchdowns. "In a sense, he was like a decoy. The defense had to pay a lot of attention to Jim Brown," Marting said.

Marting, from the stands, remembers a difference in the game being the Browns' bump-and-run coverage strategy on Berry in particular. Defensive backs would position themselves "near the line of scrimmage, and blocked Berry, holding him up for long enough to disrupt the timing of the pass pattern. That wasn't a common tactic in those days."

"The crowd went nuts, and the game ended before the clock ran out, called by the refs as thousands of fans rushed onto the field," Marting remembered. Officials let the final twenty-six seconds evaporate, and the goalposts were "demolished" at one end of the field.

Cleveland Brown quarterback Frank Ryan tosses a pass to Gary Collins in the end zone in a 1964 regular-season game. *Marvin M. Greene, the Plain Dealer.*

"I know it's corny, but it really was a magnificent team effort. The defense was just great and you've got to give them a lot of credit," Ryan said. "They've been unjustly ridiculed all year. They went into this determined to show people—and they certainly proved their point."

Shula, for his part, was blunt about the loss in postgame interviews, according to the *Plain Dealer*: "The Baltimore dressing room resembled a morgue as Don Shula surveyed the shocking defeat. 'We killed our own drives by giving up the ball on fumbles,' the disappointed but still amiable coach explained. 'I can't say anything. They beat us.'"

One account summarized the upset succinctly: "When Frank Ryan, Gary Collins, Jim Brown and Co. finished rambling over the shocked Colts 27–0 they had exposed Johnny Unitas and Lenny Moore as ordinary mortals, not super men.…The Colts had been installed as solid seven-point favorites to chase the Browns into Lake Erie."

But, of all things, it's a Victorian wedding rhyme—"Something Old, Something New, Something Borrowed, Something Blue, and a Sixpence in Her Shoe"—that comes to mind regarding a few long-lost memories surrounding the game.

SOMETHING OLD

Sports Illustrated, at the time only ten years old, covered the game. The magazine, known for its sharp, observational coverage and incredible photography over the years, had a no-brainer when it came to deciding the magazine cover that week. But the magazine made a key mistake. Instead of letting the game's actions and stars play out, it assumed that the heavily favored Colts would win and had prepared a cover portrait of Shula and Unitas. In those days, film was at a premium, and the process of covering a game on deadline was a bit arduous for photographers. (In those pre-digital days, runners were hired to ferry film back for development or mailing. One of the runners that day was Paul Drayton, who had attended Cathedral Latin High School and Villanova University. He was a two-time track medalist in the Tokyo Olympics, held months earlier.)

Two days after the game, the *Plain Dealer* even reported that the issue was coming and how many pages would be devoted to the game.

The issue carried six pages on the game, with six photos, three of which were sequential shots of Gary Collins's final touchdown reception. One is a close-up shot of a grimacing Jim Brown, uniform muddy, about to stiff-arm a defender. Another shows linebacker Vince Costello reaching for Lenny Moore of the Colts. The final shot is of Lou Groza kicking. All are in black and white. The issue also carried coverage of the American Football League championship game, held a day before the Colts-Browns game. Like the Colts-Browns coverage, the story is across six pages, with two of four photos in color.

Under the headline "Upset of the Mighty," Tex Maule's story lauded Ryan and the Browns for "one of the biggest of all football upsets." Noting that the Browns had the league's worst defense, Maule writes that the Browns grew up and came together as a cohesive unit in the win. With a descriptive flair, he described the game: "For a half, it was a spectacularly dull game. Neither team seemed willing to gamble for a long gain; Unitas and Ryan played with all the flair of a pair of elderly clubwomen in a Sunday afternoon croquet match."

Overall, it was not a bad deal for a magazine that cost thirty-five cents. The only problem was the cover. What *SI* had decided on for the cover had become old right away. It had to scramble and sub in a rather nondescript shot of the facemask-less Ryan as Baltimore's Gino Marchetti chases him. Neil Leifer, a talented photographer, took the photo. But it is, by all accounts, not a great one. Several years ago, the *Orlando Sentinel*'s Chris Harry wrote that "the lunatics at *Sports Illustrated* expected such a lopsided victory" that they had opted for the Shula-Unitas shot. The old photo had been in color; the replacement of Ryan was in black and white.

One other note about the cover: There actually was a third cover as a potential backup. The magazine's regular "Letter from the Publisher" talks about covers prepared for various issues but never run.

> *The cover at left is one you will never see on Sports Illustrated, but it might well have appeared in place of this week's action photograph from the NFL playoff. A standby, it was ready for the presses in the perfectly possible event that weather grounded the plane we had chartered to take film of Sunday's game from Cleveland to our printing facilities in Chicago. A delay of 30 minutes anywhere en route would have forced us to use the standby. There was, obviously, no delay, so the standby cover now joins a number of similar collector's items, including those below.*

The magazine then details six other covers that never ran.

The cover *SI* had waiting in the wings to use was not of a photograph but a minimalistic sketch of a player.

SOMETHING NEW

The Browns' fifth-year safety, Ross Fichtner, who had done his part in helping shut down the Colts' receivers, had a big year. In January, he and another motorist rescued two people whose car had shot over a bridge in Mantua, south of Cleveland, and landed in water. Fichtner went into the water, and he and the other motorist pulled out the victims. Then, forty-eight hours after the game against the Colts, he had a new reason to celebrate: His wife gave birth to a seven-pound, two-ounce girl.

A week before the game, amid all the coverage, a story about Jim Brown gave an indication of the football player's new career. Brown had signed a contract that called for him to appear in three movies for Paramount Pictures. Brown would play the 1965 season and then famously retire a year before his contract was up in a dispute with owner Art Modell. Modell was upset that film-production delays were causing Brown to miss part of training camp. Brown's new career would mean the end to his success on the gridiron in Cleveland.

SOMETHING BORROWED

Two weeks before the title game, the Browns traveled to New York to face the Giants. Ryan led Cleveland to a 52–20 romp. He was nearly perfect, completing twelve of thirteen passes for 202 yards and five touchdowns. For his effort, he was awarded the game ball, which he put in his locker upon his return to Cleveland.

In the postgame excitement of the Browns' locker room, someone—apparently in front of scores of people—slipped in and stole the ball, which Ryan's teammates had autographed. A team official said that if the ball was returned it would be replaced with a new ball, no questions asked. Ryan was, as his sportswriter-wife, Joan Ryan, wrote three days later, "crestfallen." "This has to be the most rotten trick ever played on me. That ball meant more to me than you could ever imagine." But the case of the missing "prized pigskin," as one paper put it, soon was solved.

It turns out that a man watching television in Syracuse, New York, spotted a sixteen-year-old in the locker room. He read about the stolen ball and, figuring the kid probably didn't have reason to be there, contacted Syracuse police, who went to the teen's home and found the ball—and

Running back Jim Brown and quarterback Frank Ryan, after the Cleveland Browns defeated the Baltimore Colts for the championship in 1964. *Richard J. Misch, the Plain Dealer.*

more. Police, who said "the youth is attracted to sports souvenirs," found a collection of memorabilia in the home, including a bat belonging to Roger Maris pilfered from the Yankees' dressing room and a helmet procured after the Pitt-Syracuse game. Amazingly, the boy was not charged for the theft of Ryan's game ball. Police said they would mail the ball to Ryan's home in Texas with an apology from the boy. Left unanswered is how, even in an age before high-security digital media credentials, did a teenager obtain a working press pass?

SOMETHING BLUE

Disappointment hit the Baltimore faithful even before the game took place. The Colts' band, which had traveled to previous title games, including the famed 1958 championship at New York, was told it could not go to Cleveland. Instead, the Browns' owner, Art Modell, had brought in Florida A&M's renowned band for a reported $18,000. Reportedly, Modell had promised NFL commissioner Pete Rozelle that the band had an exciting routine, but Rozelle was disappointed by what turned out to be a rather mundane performance, even though he also nixed the Baltimore band from traveling. Only a handful of Colt band members trekked to Cleveland.

About nine thousand Baltimore fans, decked in blue and white, were relegated to the lower deck near home plate in the stadium. That was a small percentage of visiting-team fans compared to the 2016 World Series, which drew a raucous collection of Chicagoans to Cleveland's Progressive Field. The Colts were upset before the game as well as after. About seventy police officers were on hand at the airport in Baltimore to handle a potential congratulatory mob. They weren't needed; few fans showed up.

And a Sixpence in Her Shoe

The late Casey Coleman was thirteen at the time. He would grow up to be a fixture in Cleveland radio, and his award-winning broadcaster-father, Ken Coleman, had covered the game for WDOK. The young Coleman was in the locker room postgame and saw Jim Brown toss his shoes aside. Casey saved them. Years later, when Western Reserve Historical Society opened the temporary exhibit "1964: When Browns Town Was Title Town," the cleats were on display, still caked with mud from Brown's rushes that December day fifty years earlier.

Aftermath

Eleven players from the day earned Hall of Fame honors: five Browns (Jim Brown, Lou Groza, Gene Hickerson, LeRoy Kelly and Paul Warfield) and six Colts (Raymond Berry, John Mackey, Gino Marchetti, Lenny Moore, Jim Parker and Johnny Unitas).

Winners' share was $8,000; the losers took in $5,000. Not bad, considering that in today's dollars, that translates to each player on the losing team pocketing the equivalent of more than $40,000.

Ryan went on to success off the field, no surprise considering his academic background. He spent six years as director of information systems for the House of Representatives. He also was Yale's athletic director before going to work at his alma mater, Rice University, in academic positions.

That December day, when the Browns raced off the field, was the last time the team hoisted a championship trophy. They faced Baltimore two more times in postseason play, losing 34–0 in the 1968 conference championship and 20–3 in a divisional playoff game in 1971.

10

TRAGEDY ON THE DIAMOND, PART ONE

Charles Pinkney

Years ago, a well-loved ballplayer from Cleveland was hit in the head by a pitch, a tragic ending to a promising career. And we're not talking about Ray Chapman. Charles Pinkney was born in Ashtabula and moved at a young age to Collinwood, a village before it was annexed by Cleveland. He played for East High School and other area ball clubs.

He was nicknamed "Cupid," not for romantic or Valentine's references but for his resemblance to Clarence "Cupid" Childs, who was said to have cherubic features. Childs played most of his career for the Cleveland Spiders. Childs was five feet, eight inches tall; Pinkney was five feet, six inches. Both were solid, weighing over 180 pounds. Both played second base.

Pinkney broke into the minor-league ranks in 1906 with New Castle of the Ohio-Pennsylvania League. He was seventeen. He was seen as a promising player and lived up to his billing. He hit .278 in his rookie season in professional ball, but a severely sprained ankle dropped his average to .202 in limited play in 1907. A newspaper reference in early 1908—which actually said he had to "retire"—noted that he would be back with the team, but that did not happen. Instead, Pinkney was released. He signed with Newark of the Ohio State League in 1908. In the second half of the 1909 season, he moved up to the Dayton Veterans of the Central League. Several of the league's teams, including Dayton, were suffering financial hardship, and the move amounted to what today would be called a salary dump. Players came and went through a virtual revolving door. Either way, Pinkney was in uniform for Dayton in August of that year. Affectionately referred to as a "midget" in the press because of his size, he was generally liked and seen as a speedy runner who could get on base and who had a solid glove.

Just more than a month after Pinkney joined his new team, Dayton hosted Grand Rapids in a doubleheader on September 14. Whether it was excited anticipation about his father arriving from Cleveland to watch him play, an eagerness to perform as the team closed out its season or the fact his family was planning a party for his scheduled return, Pinkney was amped up enough to hit a rare home run in the first game. Pinkney hit the shot off Casey Hageman, who two seasons later would begin a brief major-league career playing for three teams in thirty-two games. Hageman also started the second game. In the fifth inning, Charles Sr. arrived at Fairview Park and was able to say hello to his son.

In the seventh and final inning—it had been decided this would be the last inning, as the sun was fading, despite the visitors being ahead—Pinkney stepped into the batter's box to face the right-handed Hageman. Pinkney drew a 3-0 count. The fourth pitch also appeared to be a ball, as Craig Lammers's Society for American Baseball Research biography on Pinkney notes. Lammers cites the account of what happened in the *Dayton Journal*: The ball "approached the home plate like a swift shot from a rifle. It was growing very dark and before Pinkney could dodge, the ball had hit him square in the head just back of and above the left ear. The report was so loud it was heard by practically all present. The athlete fell to the ground like one shot." Players converged over home plate. The Dayton team president, Elmer Redelle, summoned doctors. One of the first people to get to the fallen player was Pinkney's father.

Pinkney was taken to St. Elizabeth Hospital, just a few miles to the south. His father, who had helped carry his twenty-year-old son to the ambulance, fainted. Pinkney Sr. was a Civil War veteran, and the team his son played for at the time of his death was so named because the ballpark was located near a hospital that had cared for veterans of the war.

Early reports said the younger Pinkney would pull through. But he slipped in and out of consciousness, and doctors performed a trephining operation, an ancient procedure in which a hole is drilled into the skull. After noon the next day, Pinkney died. More than five hundred people attended his funeral in Collinwood.

Pinkney's on-the-field death preceded Chapman's by eleven years. The two are bound by their ties to Cleveland, fatal pitches and unfortunate timing. Both are victims of simply having played before two key inventions were

Charles J. Pinkney's grave in historic Lake View Cemetery in Cleveland. His headstone makes note of his career and reads, "The umpire in the game of life called a favorite player out." *Marc Bona, cleveland.com.*

implemented that are now taken for granted: batting helmets and lights for night games. Like many inventions, neither came about instantaneously. Both underwent years of trials and tests. Batting helmets would not be mandatory in the major leagues until the 1956 season, more than a quarter century after Chapman was hit. Early lights, while rudimentary and far from perfect, were in the experimental stage when Pinkney took the field in Dayton. In fact, it was just more than a month before Pinkney's death, on July 7, 1909, that they were used when Zanesville played at Grand Rapids. It is believed to be the first night game in organized baseball. (Because of Central League rules about start times, it did not count as an official game and is seen as an exhibition.) Hageman went 18-16 on that 1909 team. The game used thirty "arcs" of light from the grandstand. This resulted in better vision for the batters than the fielders, a newspaper report stated.

Chapman had faced Carl Mays, a submarine pitcher with no qualms of throwing inside. Pinkney, though, was ahead of the count, and any pitcher behind 3-0 will look to the plate. Both pitches occurred as the sun was fading.

In his biographical portrait of Pinkney, Lammers cites the *Dayton Journal's* Julian Behr, who said the game should have been called after five innings.

Pinkney's story faded into obscurity for decades. Death on a ball field remains uncommon, but one that occurs in a minor-league game would not receive as much coverage as when Chapman—a star in the major leagues—was killed. Society wasn't as litigious, so no subsequent lawsuits were brought to light, which would have kept the story in the public eye.

Chapman and Pinkney are linked by their fatal moments on a baseball field, their well-liked personalities and the fact that they are buried in the same place: Lake View Cemetery in Cleveland. But the pitchers they faced also have an unlikely bond. Mays and Hageman lived into their seventies. But during their playing careers, each was involved in litigation concerning his career. In each case, the Boston Red Sox were involved. In 1919, Boston traded Mays to the New York Yankees. What ensued was a fight over team autonomy. It created factions among owners and resulted in a rankled league president, multiple court dates and injunctions. In the end, Mays stayed with the Yankees and won eighty games in pinstripes over five seasons. Hageman's case also swirled around autonomy, ignited by the pitcher's refusal to play for Denver of the Western League. In 1912, the Red Sox effectively sent down Hageman, but he refused to report. The question of who owned his rights wound up in court, with the Base Ball Players Fraternity suing on his behalf. The case lasted several years until Boston settled.

One hundred years after Pinkney's death, the ballplayer's story was remembered by the *Plain Dealer's* John Campanelli. He detailed Pinkney's death, but a footnote on the story mentioned that the young player had no headstone. An anonymous donor came forward and funded one.

The simple headstone reads "Died by a Pitched Baseball" and "The Umpire in the Game of Life Called a Favorite Player Out."

A final note about Charles Pinkney will remain, in all likelihood, a supposition. The Cleveland Naps reportedly were planning to bring up Pinkney. Had he not been killed on the field in Dayton in 1909, there is a chance he and Chapman would have graced the same infield, turning double plays in the seasons leading to Cleveland's famed World Series title in 1920.

II

TRAGEDY ON—AND OFF—THE DIAMOND, PART TWO

Ray Chapman's Family

I t took one pitch to end a popular ballplayer's life. It cut short a career on the field and a love affair off of it.

Many fans know that Ray Chapman was struck by a pitch on August 16, 1920, and died the following day. He was well liked by his teammates and fans. At the time of his death, he was hitting .303 on a very good Cleveland team. A speedy shortstop—he once circled the bases in fourteen seconds—he was a key component on the 1920 Indians.

And he was in love. Chapman had met Kathleen Daly, whom Mike Sowell describes in his tremendously comprehensive book *The Pitch That Killed* as "as beautiful as she was sophisticated." An Indian staffer had introduced the two, and Katy, as she was known, would arrive at the ballpark, chauffeur-driven, and sit in a box to watch "Chappie" play. She knew how to keep score. As Sowell writes, "From the beginning their romance was played out against the backdrop of baseball."

Katy was the daughter of Martin B. Daly, a prominent business executive who, like his daughter, enjoyed baseball. Daly was president of the East Ohio Gas Company.

The couple became engaged in 1918. They married on October 29, 1919, a day before Katy turned twenty-six. The ceremony was in the Dalys' East Side home on Euclid Avenue. Indian player-manager Tris Speaker, a close friend of Chapman's, was best man. One of the songs sung that night was "Believe Me, If All Those Endearing Young Charms," which contains these lyrics: "Oh! the heart, that has truly lov'd, never forgets /

But as truly loves on to the close." It turned out to foreshadow the couple's time together.

Less than a year after they married, Katy became pregnant. Martin Daly was preparing his son-in-law for a job at his company after Ray retired from baseball. That might have happened after the 1920 season.

Chapman was more than a ballplayer. He loved singing, music and theater. He kept his team loose with his singing and was a devoted family man who was looking forward to fatherhood.

But on the morning of August 16, 1920, baseball was on Chapman's mind as the temperature hit eighty degrees in New York. Cleveland, New York and Chicago were locked in a pennant race, and the Indians descended on the Polo Grounds for the opener of a three-game series with the Yankees. It would begin a fifteen-game road trip over thirteen dates. Chapman came to the plate in the top of the fifth inning, the skies overcast and Carl Mays on the mound, going for his one-hundredth career victory. The Indians were up, 3–0. Teammate Jack Graney, one of Chapman's closest pals, looked on from the bench.

What happened next has been reported and written about numerous times. The pitcher fired toward the plate and the ball bounced back toward Mays, who fielded it and threw to first base. But Chapman hadn't swung. The ball had hit him on the left side of the head. Those closest to the action were catcher Muddy Ruel and umpire Tommy Connelly. Ruel tried to grab Chapman as he fell; Connelly raced to the grandstand and called for a doctor. Chapman was rushed to a hospital, where he died at 4:40 a.m. the following day.

Fans mourned the loss of Chapman. Stages of grief set in throughout the league. Anger took root among the players, and that anger was directed at Mays and the Yankees. Mays had come up with the Red Sox with a young pitcher named Babe Ruth. He used a submarine-style motion: his right arm would dip to the ground near the pitcher's release point. The antithesis of Chapman in personality, Mays was seen as belligerent. He led the American League in 1917 with fourteen beanings. In 1918, he hit eleven batters, the second-highest total in the league. (Mays hit eighty-nine batters in his career, though that does not rank anywhere near league leaders in that category.) In 1919, he once intentionally fired a ball into the stands, hitting a fan. Personality aside, one thing that happened regarding Mays in 1919 might have changed the course of baseball history—and Chapman's life.

That season, Mays was pitching for Boston, his frustration mounting with lack of run support and what he saw as inept play from teammates. In the middle of a game he was pitching at Chicago, disgusted with his team's

Ray Chapman's grave at Lake View Cemetery. *Marc Bona, cleveland.com.*

play, he walked off the field. While his teammates strode to the bench, he went straight to the clubhouse, put on street clothes and left. That petulant fit ignited what amounted to impromptu free agency in the middle of the season for Mays's services. Several teams jumped into a bidding war. The idea of a player quitting and becoming a de facto free agent in the middle of the season was unheard of in 1919. It created factions of owners for and against American League president Ban Johnson, who was to rule on the matter.

When the dust settled, it was the Yankees who picked up Mays for $40,000 and two players. But it should be noted that one of the teams that had proposed a trade for Mays was the Cleveland Indians. Had Indian owner Jim Dunn been the most persuasive, Mays might have wound up as a teammate of Chapman's instead of being known as the man who threw the only fatal beanball in Major League Baseball history. The possibility that the Indians would have gone on to capture the 1920 World Series with Mays and without key players who reportedly were part of the deal remains, of course, speculation. But on August 16, he was on the mound in the Polo Grounds.

The immediate aftermath drew an array of emotions. Mays actually blamed Connelly, because, he claimed, the umpire had let a scuffed ball

Ray Chapman's grave at Lake View Cemetery in Cleveland is consistently adorned with artifacts remembering the fallen ballplayer. *Marc Bona, cleveland.com.*

remain in play. (The league's concern over the price of baseballs, and how long they stayed in a game, may have contributed, along with the overcast day and lack of lights, to poor visibility.)

Ray and Katy's relationship could be summed up in comments both made after he was hit. In the clubhouse, Chapman, barely able to speak, was able to ask the team trainer for his wedding ring, which was slipped on the player's hand. He smiled briefly, the simple act giving him some comfort. Before he lapsed into unconsciousness, Chapman mentioned Katy to a friend who had traveled to the game from Boston and who went in the ambulance with him. His thoughts were of reassuring his wife. Katy, meanwhile, pregnant, had traveled from Cleveland to be with Ray. When she arrived in New York, she told a priest, "I feared that something must happen. We had been too happy together, and it couldn't last." A little while later, at the hospital, her worst fears came true when she learned her husband had died.

Mays did not visit the funeral home, and with emotions running raw, that probably was a wise decision. He also did not reach out to Katy. Indian owner Jim Dunn, pitcher Joe Wood and Speaker met with reporters at the Hotel Winton after returning from New York. This was the same hotel where Chapman's bachelor dinner had been held. (The chef at the hotel was none other than Hector Boiardi, who would start a line of canned Italian food known as Chef Boyardee.)

Speaker and Graney remained so broken up that they did not attend the funeral at St. John's Cathedral in Cleveland three days later. While Katy and Ray had enjoyed a brief marriage, a love affair and the spotlight—he as a well-known ballplayer, she as the daughter of a prominent and wealthy businessman—one bit of bad blood surrounded them: Bitterness steeped in religious convictions took hold. Sowell's biography notes that a fight apparently took place between teammates Speaker, Graney and Steve O'Neill over where Chapman should be buried. Speaker, like Chapman, was Protestant. Graney and O'Neill, like Katy and her family, were Catholic. While that difference did not manifest itself between the couple, others inexplicably weighed in based on belief systems on where Chapman should be buried.

The boiled-over anger over the beaning lingered throughout the league, despite the brief time off for the Indians to attend the funeral. (The game scheduled the day after Chapman was hit was postponed, too, obviously.) On August 29, the Indians played at Washington. Reminders of the beaning hovered. Stan Coveleski was on the mound again for Cleveland. And Connelly and Dick Nallin, both of whom had worked the August 16 game, were umpires. When the Indians walked into the clubhouse, they found a handwritten message scrawled across their lockers: "Mays the murderer." (It was later found out that a clubhouse attendant had done it, though it being scrawled during a Cleveland-Washington game is odd.)

Chapman's death dominated baseball. Teams talked of boycotting the Yankees when Mays pitched. It's a wonder Cleveland kept its focus to win a tight pennant race with the Yankees and the White Sox. Less than two months after Chapman's death, Cleveland won its first World Series title, defeating Brooklyn in seven games in the best-of-nine format. Players voted to give Chapman's World Series share to his widow. It amounted to less than $4,000.

What became known as the Roaring Twenties was unkind to Katy Chapman. Rae Marie Chapman, the baby she was pregnant with at the time of Chapman's death, was born on February 27, 1921. Katy remarried in 1923, to a cousin on her mother's side, Joseph F. McMahon, an oil-business executive. They were married in East Cleveland in St. Philomena's Church—ironically, the chosen site for Ray Chapman's funeral before it was moved to St. John's. They went to Hawaii on their honeymoon and made their home in Los Angeles. On October 12, 1926, they had a son, Joseph Jr. Her son's birth came just more than a month after the death of her father, Martin.

Less than two years later, Katy and her husband were preparing for another trip to Hawaii. Not feeling well and with bags packed, she had taken some medicine and collapsed. Whether it was an accident or intentionally self-inflicted remains somewhat of a mystery, though Sowell cites a coroner's report that calls it suicide. Her hometown paper referred to her having a nervous breakdown after being released from the hospital. Rae Marie was seven at the time. The girl was sent to Cleveland to live with her grandparents. The family tried to shield the girl from a measles outbreak. Sowell cites a conversation between a nurse and the girl. At one point, Rae Marie told the nurse, "I was talking to my mother last night." The nurse thought she meant her grandmother, but Rae Marie insisted it was her own mother, who had died the previous year. Then she told the nurse: "She talks to me once in a while. And she told me I'll be with her soon." Deaths from measles had dipped in 1929, but complications arose, and Rae Marie Chapman died on April 27, 1929. Within nine years, Ray, his wife and daughter were all gone.

Neither Mays nor Chapman is in the Hall of Fame. Mays's numbers are borderline, and while a case can be made for his inclusion, it's generally thought that the combination of his reputation along with one pitch in 1920 has kept him out. Speaker, of course, is in the Hall of Fame, his .345

Martin Daly, his daughter Kathleen and Kathleen's daughter, Rae Marie, are buried near each other in Calvary Cemetery in Cleveland. Ray Chapman lies just six miles to the north in Lake View Cemetery. *Marc Bona.*

Lake View Cemetery is the final resting place for many historic figures, from John D. Rockefeller to Eliot Ness and others, including Ray Chapman. *Marc Bona.*

average good for sixth all-time. Before he died, he would share an unsought connection with his close friend, Chappie. In his retirement, Speaker, doing some work at his Shaker Heights home, fell from the second-story porch. One of his injuries was a fractured skull.

Ray Chapman, on the way to the ballpark for the final time in 1920, keeping his teammates relaxed, sang "Dear Old Pal of Mine," a World War I song that contains these lyrics:

> *All my life is empty, since I went away*
> *Skies don't seem to be so clear*
> *May some angel sentry, guard you while I stray*
> *And fate be kind to join us some sweet day.*

After Ray Chapman died, Katy Chapman never attended another baseball game.

12

PANTHERS AND PAPERS

I f it weren't for the threat of a lawsuit and the suggestion of a newspaper writer, fans today wouldn't be cheering the Cleveland Browns or know about the team's rich history under one of the sport's greatest coaches, Paul Brown. Instead, a coach from the college ranks would have been chosen to lead the nascent team, the Cleveland Panthers.

In 1945, the team actually was briefly known as the Panthers, and the influence of a local newspaper helped set the tone for the city's entry in the All-America Football Conference (AAFC).

The Cleveland Rams had just left town for Los Angeles, and the city was left without a football team. Chicago native Arthur McBride became the first owner of the Browns. He reached out to the public to name the team, offering a $1,000 war bond in 1945 as a prize. A U.S. Navy man wrote a forty-nine-word letter suggesting "Panthers." The nickname actually wasn't that original. Two decades earlier, it had been the name for Cleveland's football team in the first professional league. Owned by a local businessman, Charles Zimmerman, the Panthers—which had gone from a semipro team to professional in 1926 before reverting to the semipro level—played its few games in Luna Park. The East Side park was known as "Cleveland's fairyland of pleasure." The connection to "Panthers" might not have been fresh in memories, but it was less than twenty years old when McBride held his contest. War bond paid, McBride tried to move on to other team business.

But hold on: George T. Jones, who had been secretary of the old Panthers during its brief stint (five games) as a professional team, sued McBride, claiming he had rights to the name. McBride at first considered keeping it, but his new coach, Paul Brown, did not like the name Panthers, saying it was associated with a failed team. McBride refused to pay Jones and went back to the public. A Euclid man submitted the name *Browns* and received another $1,000 war bond. (Rumors persisted for years that the Browns' name was derived from Joe Louis, the "Brown Bomber" and heavyweight champion when the AAFC was being formed, but that has been disproven. The team is indeed named after the coach.) So the name *Panthers* existed for two months in 1945 before being displaced.

How Brown got the job in the first place is where John Dietrich comes in. The *Plain Dealer* sportswriter had covered a variety of teams over his career, which lasted forty-one years. He was well-versed in football, having followed the Cleveland Rams during their tenure in the 1930s and '40s. As a matter of fact, he was in a meeting during which the name was being determined, giving his stamp of approval for the succinct nickname that would fit well in tight newspaper headline counts, a frequent consideration of the time. Described as a cigar-chomping and diehard Ohioan, Dietrich was familiar with Paul Brown. At the time, Brown, the Ohio State coach, was leading the football team at the Great Lakes Navy Training Center in Chicago, a wartime stint for him.

McBride was not a football man, preferring boxing and baseball. His son, though, was attending Notre Dame, whose football team was coached by Frank Leahy. Junior's affinity for Irish football passed to the elder McBride, who traveled to see Notre Dame games across the country. When he sought a coach, his initial target was Leahy. But McBride, knowing of Dietrich's prominence in sports circles, sought the writer's advice on who to hire. Brown, came the answer. (Leahy has an indirect connection to Cleveland. The coach had a very successful eleven-year run at Notre Dame, compiling an 87-11-9 record. He never coached in the professional ranks, though he did serve in the front office of the Los Angeles Chargers in 1960. But early in his career, he served as a line coach for the Fordham Rams, whose famed "Seven Blocks of Granite" included future Green Bay Packer coaching legend Vince Lombardi. When the Cleveland Rams were being named, it was Fordham's team that served as inspiration.)

Paul Brown had gone from coaching his alma mater, Massillon Washington High School, to Ohio State, a now almost unheard-of leap in coaching ranks. Known for his pioneering marks on the game and string of successful seasons, Brown was an easy choice for Dietrich, obviously familiar with more coaching hopefuls than was McBride. The owner

Quarterback Otto Graham led some of the greatest Cleveland Brown teams ever, with Paul Brown as coach. *Plain Dealer file photo.*

then ran the choice by Arch Ward, another newspaper veteran. Ward, sports editor of the *Chicago Tribune*, had created the All-America Football Conference and had known McBride from their Chicago days. Ward gave his stamp of approval, an offer was made and Brown became coach of the new franchise in Cleveland.

McBride himself has a tie to newspapers. At a young age—some accounts say he was six—he began hawking papers on Chicago streets. He soon initiated a profitable side venture. McBride positioned himself at a busy intersection, where his customers would give him streetcar transfers they did not need for a free paper, saving them a penny. McBride would sell streetcar transfers for three cents to folks who would have had to pay a nickel. He eventually moved on to work in the circulation departments of several newspapers. In 1913, he became circulation director of the *Cleveland News*.

So, the influence of newspapermen helped put in place the foundation for the early years of the franchise.

But it was McBride's main business venture—owning taxicab companies—that would become his calling card and lead to a long-standing tradition in the NFL.

Long before ride-sharing companies like Uber and Lyft came along, taxicabs in urban areas were a regular form of transportation. In 1930, McBride resigned from the *Cleveland News* and moved to the taxicab business. He owned Zone Cab Company and, in 1931, acquired Yellow Cab Company. (He also owned a horse-racing odds publication, which led to his indictment on a conspiracy charge by a federal grand jury in 1940.)

But as a taxicab-company magnate, McBride's approach was to offer low-cost fares for the markets in which he operated. His cabs were the first ones outside of New York "to be equipped with radios." He expanded his taxicab empire to Akron, Canton and other cities. He made a point of hiring female drivers during World War II and even went so far as to buy seventy-eight acres located seven air miles east of Cleveland for the "Yellow Helicopter Taxi Service."

Here's how his taxicab business and football team came together. McBride stacked his team with as many good players as possible, but too many for the roster. So he came up with the idea to have the extra players work out with the team but be paid as employees of his cab company. That's where the term *taxi squad* originates in professional football. The term has given way over the years to "practice squad," where players do exactly that: They can practice with their team but not play in games. It's really an auxiliary developmental squad that helps the players as much as the teams. Over the years, the NFL has regulated the number of players allowed on the squad. It's invaluable to teams that, in a pinch, can call up a player who will already know offensive or defensive schemes, thereby shortening the learning curve. For the 2019 season, practice-squad players had to receive at least $8,000 per week during the season.

On a lighter note, Brownie the Elf, who has fallen in and out of favor with Brown management over the years, made his debut in 1946 on the cover of the twenty-five-cent program for the team's AAFC debut against Miami. The determined-looking elf is running with the ball, ready to stiff-arm defenders. It was the *Plain Dealer* that popularized the elf in its pages over the years, thanks to Dick Dugan. The longtime graphics artist frequently drew the scowling mascot.

"If the Browns won a game, Brownie elf was seen smiling, but if the team lost, the elf would appear battered and bruised with a black eye," one account reads. Dugan is often attributed as the originating source for Brownie. While possible, it seems unlikely. Dugan, born in 1926, enlisted at age eighteen in the U.S. Navy, where he spent two and a half years and then moved to Pittsburgh. He began teaching cartooning in Cleveland in 1947, when the Browns were already in their second season. He worked at the *Plain Dealer* from 1962 to 2000.

The Browns, under McBride, would go on to have several successful seasons in the days of the AAFC and early years in the NFL. He sold the team in 1953 for $600,000. To put that number in perspective, for the 2020 season, each player on the Browns' roster made more than that annually. What would have happened if McBride hadn't backed down from the legal challenge over the team's initial name, or if he hadn't sought the influence of the city's newspaper? Fans could be watching the Cleveland Panthers, and Paul Brown might have made his mark elsewhere.

13

BABE RUTH AND CLEVELAND

Yankee Stadium was known as the "House That Ruth Built," but Cleveland's League Park was like a second home. It's where some of Babe Ruth's most famous home runs were hit and where milestones were achieved. And it wasn't just the park that contributed to etching his name in the record books. Many moments came against the Indians in New York as well.

When Ruth came on the baseball scene, home runs were not the focus of fans or fodder for highlight reels. In fact, when Ruth slugged a Bert Cole pitch in the top of the eighth over right field in Detroit on July 18, 1921, he became the all-time home-run leader. His 139th home run had surpassed Roger Connor. The likeable Connor was a rare big man in the game in his time, at six feet, three inches and 220 pounds. Interestingly, over eighteen seasons, Connor never led the league in home runs. The most he ever hit in one campaign was 17 in 1887. Connor has been relegated to a trivia question: Who did Babe Ruth pass to become the all-time home-run leader? At the time of this writing, Connor sits tied for 601st among players on the all-time list with José Cardinal, Matt Lawton, Bill Mazeroski, Daniel Murphy and Earl Williams. Ruth, though, would hold the title for more than half a century, until April 8, 1974, when Henry Aaron hit his 715th. Ruth remains entrenched in third place in career home runs. Judging by the current players on the list, that position seems fairly safe for years to come.

Ruth hit 92 home runs off Cleveland pitchers. Of his 714 total, more than half—367—came on the road, and 46 were in Cleveland. He hit the

Left: Roger Connor is the answer to a trivia question: Who did Babe Ruth surpass to become the home-run leader? *Benjamin K. Edwards Collection via Library of Congress.*

Right: Jack Graney transitioned from a solid playing career in Cleveland to the announcing booth. *Plain Dealer file photo.*

most by any visiting player in League Park. (Ruth never hit a home run in Cleveland Municipal Stadium, a cavernous antithesis to the quaint League Park bandbox.) He victimized Stan Coveleski five times, four when the pitcher played for Cleveland. The hurler was one of nine eventual Hall of Famers who served home runs to Ruth.

But before Ruth terrorized any opposing pitcher with his power at the plate, he was a pitcher, and a good one, having amassed a 94-46 record in ten seasons. His first time on the mound came on July 11, 1914, when the nineteen-year-old Ruth faced Cleveland in the two-year-old Fenway Park. The first batter to step into the box against him was Jack Graney, who was in the middle of his fourteen-year career spent entirely with Cleveland. He singled against Ruth, whose debut was highly anticipated. At the plate, the first pitcher to throw in a major-league game against Ruth was Willie Mitchell, who struck him out in the second inning. Ruth went seven innings, allowed eight hits and finished with a 4–3 win.

But it was Cleveland where Ruth made his mark with his bat. Now, the area around East Sixty-Sixth Street and Lexington Avenue is a quiet neighborhood in the shadow of downtown Cleveland. It's romantic to think, if anyone drives along Lexington Avenue, that it once was a bustling intersection, fans dodging multiple crisscrossing trolley lines bordering the old stadium. On June 5, 1918, Ruth hit his first home run against a Cleveland pitcher, a shot "high over the right-field screen" off Johnny Enzmann in the top of the sixth. It was Ruth's seventh home run of the year and sixteenth in his career. The Indians beat the Red Sox, 5–4, in ten innings.

Right field in League Park became a target for Ruth. In the book *League Park: 1891–1946*, Ken Krsolovic and Bryan Fritz call the right-field wall "inviting" for left-handed hitters. It was a mere 290 feet from home plate. (For comparison's sake, right field at Boston's Fenway Park is the shallowest in the majors today, at 302 feet.) Any photo taken from above when League Park was around shows the stadium dropped in the middle of a residential neighborhood. The park fits snugly, as some of the property owners refused to sell homes when it was being built.

Many of Babe Ruth's prodigious home runs came in League Park. *Detroit Publishing Company via Library of Congress.*

While much has been written about Ruth as a hitter and a pitcher, it should be noted that his outfield position was determined by the "geographic orientation of the ballpark in which he was playing." While playing left field in the Polo Grounds in 1922, Ruth had lost a ball in the sun. From that point, he played right field in four stadiums, including League Park, and left field in five parks.

On July 18, 1919, Boston came to town as pressure was mounting for Cleveland manager Lee Fohl. The Red Sox beat the Naps, 8–7, in the first game of a doubleheader as Ruth had a field day with Cleveland pitching: He had a six-RBI game while slamming two home runs. It was the last game Fohl ever managed for Cleveland. It also was the last season Ruth played for Boston. He would be famously sold to the Yankees, where he would begin a long, storied career in 1920.

On June 13, 1920, Ruth hit his first home run as a Yankee against Cleveland. League Park set an attendance record that day as 29,266 came out to the stadium. They might have been entertained by Ruth's performance, which included a shot to right field in the top of the sixth inning off Elmer Myers, but the outcome was disappointing: New York pasted Cleveland, 14–0. Two months later, on August 9, Cleveland owner Jim Dunn celebrated what he called "Golden Year of Baseball Day" at the ballpark, marking half a century of professional baseball in the city as New York and Cleveland opened a key series.

Scores of former ballplayers filled the park. A twelve-foot floral wreath shaped like a bat was presented to Ruth for his mark of forty-one home runs. It was an odd moment of sportsmanship; the teams were locked in a pennant race. The Yankees won the opener, 6–3, and Ruth, upset over a poor performance at the plate, left the wreath behind for fans to scavenge its flowers. "It was too heavy," Ruth said. "I could not swing it." Exactly one week later, the teams faced each other in New York, and this time, circumstances would not be as lighthearted. That day, with Ruth on the field, Ray Chapman was hit by a pitch. He died the next day.

On August 23, 1921, Ruth faced Cleveland's Ray Caldwell. Ruth hit two home runs and finished the day with four RBIs. The first was Ruth's 150th of his career. Before the game, Ruth spent time at Oakwood Golf Club in Cleveland Heights watching the Western Open, but not playing, saying he had to save himself for baseball that day. Writers, knowing about Ruth's diversion to the course, said he "golfed the ball so high" with hyperbolic estimates of the hit: "Unofficial surveyors of the air declare Babe's first circuit clout yesterday traveled 840 feet—250 up, 250 down and 240 feet from the plate to the spot where the ball dropped in Lexington Avenue. They also estimate that had the Cleveland Discount building been located in right field at Dunn Field (*sic*), the ball Babe hit would have hit the sign that surmounts the tallest office building in Cleveland." The math didn't add up, but it was the writers' way of saying it was a towering shot.

In the third inning, "Babe swung and like a bullet the ball cleared the right field wall, hit the roof of a house across Lexington avenue, smashed a few shingles and bounded high in the air again."

(One of the umpires that day was George Moriarty, whose grandson Michael Moriarty portrayed Henry "Author" Wiggen in the 1973 film *Bang the Drum Slowly*. The team his character plays for is the New York Mammoths, with uniforms resembling the Yankees of the era.)

One pitcher who had success against Ruth was George Uhle. In 110 at-bats, Ruth reportedly hit only four home runs. But the two were friendly enough for Uhle to invite Babe to his home during a trip to Cleveland for the slugger. Years later, Uhle remembered the encounter clearly.

> *The Babe was a pip. Most of the stories about him are unprintable. I'll tell you one you can write. At the end of one season he came to Cleveland to play in a charity golf tournament and I invited him to our house for dinner. I knew about his appetite. I got a keg of beer and about a barrel of pig's knuckles and sauerkraut, his favorite food.*
>
> *He ate 'em so fast he was throwing pieces of bone over his shoulder. I didn't find out until later that my daughter, Marilyn, who was about seven at the time, was charging the kids in the neighborhood 10 cents apiece to look through the window to watch the Babe.*

Another pitcher who fared well against Ruth was Cleveland's Joe Shaute, who struck out the home-run king thirty times. But on June 7, 1928, Ruth smacked a ball off Shaute in the ninth as the Yankees added to their lead. Before the game, the slugger—known for his affinity for children—had attended a Cathedral Latin High School fundraiser carnival. He bought ice cream for a few girls, signed dozens of autographs and played a game in which you tossed a rope hoop around a live duck's head. (Ruth won the duck and gave it to a boy.) The ball, which had bounded into the street, was retrieved by a young salesman named Connie Long, who had Ruth sign it. It remained in Long's family in Cleveland for decades and was part of a display at the Baseball Heritage Museum on the home run's ninetieth anniversary. The museum sits on the site of League Park.

Just more than a month later, on July 15, the Yankees met the Indians again, this time in New York. Ruth smacked his 450th home run off George Grant, who would finish the season 10-8—his only winning season in a seven-year, 15-20 career. The *Plain Dealer* made no mention of 450 but said that Ruth had a "typical" day in which he hit a home run as his average "took a downward slide" to .310. The two-run shot came in the first inning. At the time, Ruth was in the second season of a three-year contract worth $70,000 annually. That salary holds the approximate purchasing power in early 2021 of more than $1 million.

The attention to Ruth's home runs over the 1928 season was due to the fact he had hit a record sixty in 1927, a mark that stood for thirty-four years until Roger Maris, also wearing pinstripes, broke it with sixty-one in 1961 in a well-publicized race with Mickey Mantle. It was a home-run chase before such a thing was a media phenomenon. Ruth finished the 1928 season with fifty-four home runs. Only Barry Bonds, Mark McGwire and Sammy Sosa would hit more in a single season. (The second-base umpire that day was Roy Van Graflin. Four years later, he had a front-row seat to one of Ruth's most famous home runs, the reported "called shot" in the 1932 World Series.)

Ruth's 500th blast came in Cleveland, bookended by home runs the day before and the day after. Before the game on August 11, he told the head of police at the park, "Listen I'm going to hit No. 500 today and I'll tell you what I wish you'd do. I wish you'd find the kid who gets the ball and bring him to me. I'd kinda like to save that one." He swung at Willis Hudlin's first pitch and sent it to his favorite place: deep right. Hudlin wound up with a 6–5 win in a hard-fought game, but it was Ruth's exploits that, as usual, shined. The *New York World* famously tabbed the home run "a symbol of American greatness." For years, there was a discrepancy about whether a youngster or a man caught the ball, but it appears to have been the latter. Jake Geiser from New Philadelphia retrieved it, met the Babe and got an autographed ball and $20. The bat Ruth used that day sold at auction in 2019 for $1.09 million.

Bill Dinneen, a pitcher-turned-umpire working first base that day, had several encounters with Ruth during his career. In 1922, he ejected Ruth for vile language. In 1927, he was the home-plate umpire for Ruth's 60th home run, and in 1932, he was an umpire in the called-shot game. It's also interesting to note how far ahead Ruth was to his peers in home runs. The day Ruth hit his 500th, Philadelphia slugger Cy Williams was in second place with 249. Williams finished his career with 251.

On a warm day at League Park on June 15, 1930, Ruth faced the intriguingly named Beveric Benton "Bill" Bean. Ruth had walked in his first four trips to the plate. With the Yankees ahead, 13–3, and two out in the sixth, the rookie hurler served up a pitch to Ruth, who slammed it to center field for his 537th home run. "The fifth time he lugged his big bludgeon into action he blasted out one of the most colossal home runs ever witnessed in this or any other ball park," according to a newspaper account. That hyperbole would stand. Five years later, just months after Ruth played his final game, *Plain Dealer* columnist James Doyle wrote that he considered the shot off Bean to be Ruth's longest home run in Cleveland. The teams combined for thirty-three hits, including four home runs, in the Yankees' 17–10 win. Bill McGowan, the home-plate umpire this day, had once thrown out Babe Ruth—in a spring-training game. It was McGowan's first year as a major-league ump. McGowan was quoted by sportswriter Shirley Povich as saying, "I know who you are and I know your reputation, but when I'm wearing this blue suit you're just another ball player. Get out."

Incidentally, the press was beginning to run tallies of how many home runs were hit the previous day, with league leaders and totals. It was long before fantasy baseball but proof that the age of the long ball had arrived.

Ruth continued adding to his home-run record that season. Later in June, he hit three more off of Cleveland, including one off of Sal Gliatto in Yankee Stadium. For his entire career, Gliatto threw fifteen innings in eight games, and the only home run he served was to the Babe. A month later, on July 20, 1930, Ruth took Milt Shoffner to deep right for his 550th home run. Exactly a year to the day earlier, Shoffner had made his major-league debut in League Park, also against the Yankees. He drew a full count on Ruth, then struck him out. "The crowd erupted. After the game, the Babe said to Shoffner, 'Kid, bet you never heard such applause for a man striking out.'"

On September 17, 1933, in Yankee Stadium, Cleveland great Mel Harder faced Ruth, now in the twilight of his career. Ruth recorded his thirtieth home run of the season. It was his third and final home run off of Harder. On September 16, 1934, Ruth would face Harder again in what would be the slugger's final appearance in Cleveland.

It would be nice to say that Ruth said goodbye to Cleveland and League Park on a blast to right field, but it wasn't to be. Ruth had entered the game as a pinch-hitter in the eighth inning batting ninth, a far cry from his starting days, when he often batted third ahead of Lou Gehrig. This day, he lined a Harder pitch to first baseman Hal Trosky, who knocked it down and fielded it, beating "the painfully limping" Ruth before fifteen thousand fans. He was taken out immediately. Amazingly, Ruth—thirty-nine years old—was hitting .293 at the time. A footnote on the story comes years later, when Trosky's grandson told a reporter about another encounter he had with Ruth in 1933. It was Trosky's first game in Yankee Stadium: "Babe Ruth had just got on base. Like a first baseman does, grandpa went to hold Ruth on. But Ruth said, 'I'd back up kid. I'm not going anywhere. And if you don't this next guy is going take your head off.' The next guy up was Lou Gehrig. Sure enough, Gehrig hit a liner so hard that it took grandpa's glove into right field. Ruth got to third and gave grandpa a nod like he was saying, 'Told you so.'"

Ruth retired in 1935, but Cleveland's connection to the Yankee great doesn't end there. On June 13, 1948, Ruth—a shell of his former self, suffering from cancer—appeared at Yankee Stadium on a rainy day. Ceremonies were held marking the twenty-fifth anniversary of Yankee Stadium and the retirement of his number 3 jersey. He needed help to put on his uniform. Photographer Nat Fein of the *New York Daily News* was dispatched to the stadium to cover the festivities. Fein captured one of the most iconic photos in American sports history, angling around a band playing "Auld Lang Syne" to capture the Babe from behind. Ruth is using a bat as a cane as he stands in the stadium, his stadium, as almost fifty thousand fans look on.

The bat he used belonged to Cleveland's greatest pitcher, Bob Feller. He had grabbed it as he walked up the dugout steps.

The Yankees had lost three in a row to Cleveland and were about to play the fourth and final game of the three-day series. Fittingly for New York, the Yankees won, 5–3.

It would be nice to say that some of the Babe's magic rubbed off on Feller that day at the plate, but the pitcher went 0-2 and took the loss. The Indians play-by-play radio announcer that season was Jack Graney, who thirty-four years earlier had become the first man on a major-league diamond to dig in his cleats in a batter's box against Ruth.

The picture would be known as *The Babe Bows Out*. Fein would win a Pulitzer Prize.

Two months later, Ruth died.

14

THE FIRST PASS

On December 16, 2019, New Orleans Saint quarterback Drew Brees raced back a few yards, quickly turned to his left and threw a pass to tight end Josh Hill for a five-yard touchdown against Indianapolis. It was his 540th TD pass—points for fantasy football players everywhere and good enough for Brees to become the NFL's leader in touchdown passes.

The yardage quarterbacks rack up has grown to astounding proportions over the years. Each of the four leading QBs in passing yardage has thrown for more than seventy thousand yards. Each has thrown for the equivalent of more than forty miles. Professional football has been around for more than one hundred years, its roots on the ground with grind-it-out runners and blood-and-guts blocking and tackling. The passing game evolved and shines in modern-day football with aerial attacks the norm, not the exception. Many years ago, though, the forward pass was as novel as the look of the game and leather helmets. And it turns out that Drew Brees, Tom Brady and all those fantasy players have a Clevelander named George "Peggy" Parratt to thank.

The genesis of the forward pass can be found in rule changes that came about in 1905. Passes had been made—illegally—for years. But the game's violence led to a secret summit, with Teddy Roosevelt acting as catalyst. In 1905, eighteen players were killed playing football at various levels. Rules were enacted for both semblance of order in the game and safety of players. One of those changes made the forward pass legal.

Cleveland Brown linebacker Genard Avery and defensive back Jabrill Peppers pressure New Orleans Saint quarterback Drew Brees in a 2018 game. Brees is the NFL's all-time leader in passing yards. *Joshua Gunter, cleveland.com.*

At that time, however, the passing game did not resemble the air-it-out type of attack that teams employ today. In fact, the rules in place didn't really encourage the pass at all. To legally pass the ball, the thrower had to be at least five yards behind the line of scrimmage. The penalty if this rule was not adhered to was a turnover to the defense. The rules even stipulated that if a pass was incomplete and untouched by either team, the ball would turn over to the defense.

The first legal pass was thrown in college the following season. On September 5, 1906, St. Louis University quarterback Bradbury Robinson attempted to pass in a game against Carroll College in Waukesha, Wisconsin. As is the case with many inventions and historic achievements, the first time was unsuccessful. It fell incomplete and, because of the game's early rules, resulted in a turnover. But Robinson—who was born in Bellevue, Ohio, about seventy miles west of Cleveland—would not be deterred. With the game tied, 0–0, Robinson connected with Jack Schneider, and college football had its first completed pass. St. Louis won, 22–0, ushering in the pass and making an all-ground game obsolete. Robinson, who would become a doctor and a two-term mayor in Minnesota, led his team to an undefeated season at 11-0. His longest pass that year was sixty-seven yards, impressive considering that the ball's shape was rounder than what is used today and not conducive to passing. Robinson's coach, Eddie Cochems, deserves some of the credit. He saw the potential of the passing game despite the ball's shape resembling that of a watermelon. He had the foresight to believe the pass would be a game-changer, and he and his willing quarterback prepared before the season.

Then, on October 25, the professional ranks ushered in the forward pass. It was a natural progression, as Pro Football Hall of Fame archivist Jon Kendle notes, as the college rules acted as the basis for the professional game at the time. (What became the NFL would not be established until 1920.) Parratt quarterbacked the Massillon Tigers against a combined team from Benwood and Moundsville, West Virginia, cities on the Ohio River. It was a short pass to Dan Policowski, who went by the name Dan "Bullet" Riley. (Aliases were common for masking professional status or other reasons.) The moment did not merit flashy headlines; the pass did not figure into the scoring of the game, a rout of either 60–0 or 61–0, depending on accounts. And Parratt—an exceptional athlete—was noted for a ninety-five-yard touchdown run during the game, which was played in Massillon. While the game looked different from today's, at least one thing stayed the same: The West Virginia team apparently argued with the officials throughout the game.

Parratt's pass might have remained a forgotten footnote, but he was an early star on the field and a huge influencer off of it. Born in Cleveland, he was a three-sport standout for Case who moonlighted under the name "Jimmy Murphy" playing professional football for a team in Shelby in Richland County. But when officials at his college confronted him, he admitted to the violation of amateur status, and his college baseball, basketball and football careers were over. Accounts of Parratt on a field or court usually effused hyperbole: "Ducking, dodging, whirling, shooting across the floor, the team captained by 'Peggy' Parratt played a game that can truly be styled wonderful. As one man the five played, working the ball from one end to the other of the long gymnasium." He coached baseball at Case, quarterbacked the Massillon Tigers and refereed football games. In 1916, he served as a rare quadrumvirate; he was owner, general manager, coach and quarterback of the Akron Indians. In his playing days, he weighed a now unthinkable 168 pounds.

Parratt even competed in an athletic-club handball tournament in 1925, losing in the semifinal, when he was forty-one. After his playing career, he was a relentless sports promoter, even trying to bring in the "Flying Finn," Paavo Nurmi, one of the greatest Olympians and long-distance runners, for a track event in Cleveland. He also became an exceptional bridge player.

George W. "Peggy" Parratt is buried in Cleveland's Lake View Cemetery. *Marc Bona.*

Parratt's accomplishments are as forgotten as a reoccurring screen pass that gains a few yards today. In 1913, seven years after his pioneering throw, a pair of Notre Dame teammates took jobs at Cedar Point amusement park, working as lifeguards, clerks and restaurant checkers. In their limited free time, they tossed around a football, working late to draw up passing plays and then running them on the beach. The players were quarterback Gus Dorais and end Knute Rockne. That year, Notre Dame defeated Army, 35–13, on the strength of a balanced run-pass attack never seen before. Dorais completed fourteen of seventeen passes for 243 yards. As Notre Dame University historians note, it was the moment the pass "revolutionized the game, and the victory that put Notre Dame football on the national map."

But the beginnings of the pass, now an integral—and virtually required—part of the game, are due to Peggy Parratt.

Parratt earned engineering and law degrees and worked in Cleveland for the Ohio Crankshaft Company. When he died on January 3, 1959, his obituary noted his football career, work life and even bridge accomplishments. But there is no mention of his pass on October 25, 1906.

15

Larry Twitchell's Special Day

On a surprisingly cool August afternoon, Larry Twitchell had a career day with the Cleveland Spiders. His career, while not Hall of Fame fodder, lends itself to a collection of assorted milestones. Twitchell became one of the first major leaguers—and the first for a Cleveland team—to accomplish one of baseball's rarest feats: hitting for the cycle. It's one of a few distinctions the ballplayer holds.

Twitchell was born in Cleveland during the Civil War years and became a nineteenth-century precursor of Shohei Ohtani, the Anaheim Angel player who doubles as a pitcher and designated hitter. Twitchell came up as a pitcher with the National League's Detroit Wolverines in 1886. He went 17-11 while hitting .263. He played for six teams in three leagues.

On August 15, 1889, with temperatures in the sixties, Cleveland unloaded on Boston pitcher Kid Madden. Two years earlier, Madden had won twenty-one games in his rookie year. But on this day in Cleveland, he didn't have his stuff. The Spiders walloped the Beaneaters, 19–8. Madden, a slight left-hander, went the distance in a game that saw all but one Cleveland player get at least one hit. Most had a multiple-hit game as the Spiders scored in every inning. They collected twenty-seven hits. But it was Twitchell in particular who lit up Madden, spraying balls to all parts of the field.

Batting cleanup, he started in the first inning with a single to left field. In the third, he banged out a triple off the wall in left and followed that with another triple to center in the fourth. He doubled in the sixth inning to right-center and hit a home run to left-center an inning later. In the ninth inning, he capped his day with a triple to center field. He finished six-for-six with a walk and accounted for sixteen total bases. He is one of only thirteen players to have five extra-base hits in a game.

Of the players who have hit for the cycle, Twitchell is the only player who also pitched in his game. He relieved starter Jersey Bakely early and went one inning, yielding a walk and no hits or runs. He then moved back to his left-field position.

Hitting for the cycle remains a rarity; only 330 major-league players have done it through 2020. The first player to accomplish it was Irish-born Curry Foley, playing for the Buffalo Bisons in 1882. He did it against the Cleveland Blues. Foley remains the only player to have both a grand slam and a natural reverse cycle (home run, triple, double, single in that order). The term *cycle* is believed to date to 1921 but would not become part of baseball's lexicon until the 1930s. The phenomenon has included twenty-four inside-the-park home runs, astounding when you think there are about 165,000 at-bats

Larry Twitchell played his first three seasons with Detroit. He would play for the Cleveland Spiders in 1889 and the Cleveland Infants in 1890. He had a memorable game in 1889 for the Spiders, hitting for the cycle. *Benjamin K. Edwards Collection via Library of Congress.*

per season. A grand slam has been included in a player's cycle nine times, and the cycle has been done in natural order—single, double, triple and home run—fourteen times. Twice, both in the nineteenth century, the same players hit cycles just seven days apart. Cincinnati's John Reilly did it two times in 1883, and Tip O'Neill of the St. Louis Browns notched a pair of cycles in 1887 in a week that incredibly saw another cycle, by Pittsburgh's Fred Carroll. Incidentally, in 1887, Twitchell's salary was $1,200.

After Twitchell, nine players wearing Cleveland uniforms achieved the feat (Twitchell was the only one not playing for what is now the Indians). Cleveland native Bill Bradley did it 1903. Earl Averill became one of a record eight players to hit for the cycle in the 1933 season. He and Twitchell are the only players to do it in Cleveland; the others were all on the road. Cleveland players who grace the box score with a cycle range from the lesser-known Odell Hale in 1938 to Hall of Famer Larry Doby in 1952. Tony Horton and

Andre Thornton each accomplished it in the 1970s. In 2003, Travis Hafner did it in Minnesota the day millions were affected by the Northeast blackout. Rajai Davis did it in 2016, the year the Indians went to the World Series, and Jake Bauers hit for the cycle on June 14, 2019.

Two years after his big day, Twitchell was playing for Columbus of the American Association. The 1891 season was winding down, and Milwaukee transferred its final series to Minneapolis. On October 2, Milwaukee "hosted" Columbus, beating the Solons from Ohio's capital city, 5–0.

It turned out to be one of the final games for the league, which folded soon after. Twitchell, batting cleanup, went 0-3 as Milwaukee pitcher Frank Killen allowed six hits, two walks and struck out four. The teams were supposed to play the following day, but cold weather forced a postponement. They traveled back to Milwaukee, and Columbus lost again. That turned out to be the final game for both teams. But the significance of the October 2 game, in which Twitchell played, remains a regional historical footnote: It is the only major-league game played in the state of Minnesota before the Twins came to town in 1961. (The year 1891 would be the final season for Madden, whom Twitchell had victimized in his cycle game. He went 13-12 and finished his career 54-50. Five years later, he died of tuberculosis. He was twenty-nine.)

Larry Twitchell, shown as a pitcher when he was with Detroit. *Benjamin K. Edwards Collection via Library of Congress.*

Twitchell's final year as a player was 1894, a season when he also was pressed into service as an umpire after being released during the season. The following two seasons, he managed the Milwaukee Brewers. A rare fit of poignant honesty from a manager about his team came in Twitchell's first year at the helm. A sportswriter in Indianapolis wrote, "Owing to some misfortunes attending the team, he [Twitchell] expected to win only one of the two games scheduled here." That prompted a flowery though biting sarcastic commentary from the writer: "After the games played by Milwaukee a suspicion as strong as the odor of young onions without parsley settled upon the worshipful that Mr. Twitchell would do well to take his club home, cancel all scheduled dates for a week

Larry Twitchell is buried in Lakewood Park Cemetery in Rocky River. *Marc Bona.*

and teach it to play ball." Milwaukee was 9-13 at the time and would finish in sixth place with a record of 57-67. The next season saw another sixth-place finish, and that was the end of Twitchell's managerial career.

Twitchell also was part of a phenomenon known as "heaving contests" or "distance throwing." Players would engage in competitions to see who could throw a baseball the farthest. The contests took place in the nineteenth century and into the first half of the twentieth. On multiple occasions, a player named John Hatfield threw a ball more than 400 feet. On a late July day in 1893 in Augusta, Georgia, Twitchell bested Hatfield by two yards with a throw of 135 yards, 2 feet and 2 inches—more than 407 feet. Twitchell is one of several players over the years to hold a record in this competition, whose popularity eventually waned. (The record is believed to be held by Glen Gorbous, who had a brief career in the 1950s with two major-league teams. On August 1, 1957, he threw a ball 445 feet, 10 inches. That's the equivalent of about one and a half football fields.) Such contests will remain passing trends of the times, unless amateurs want to give it a go. Players and team owners alike would frown on the potential for injury.

In Twitchell's retirement, he lived on West Boulevard in Cleveland and continued to play baseball in a church league. A 1916 newspaper feature said he was playing well, doing so alongside his sons, ages twenty-four and twenty-two. In 1927, at age sixty-three, he played at Dunn Field in a fathers-and-sons benefit game for Charlie Smith, a former player who had suffered a sunstroke.

In 1912, the *Plain Dealer* chose Cleveland's twenty best ballplayers of all time. Larry Twitchell made the list. "Although he retired many, many years ago, Larry could go out next summer and probably bat better than some of the outfielders who will draw their salaries in the major league circles. His eye is as keen as ever, but his speed is gone."

Three years after the benefit game, Twitchell died. He is buried in Lakewood Park Cemetery in Rocky River.

16

The Birth of the Slider

When a pitcher takes the mound, he does so with an arsenal at his disposal. Cutters, two-seam fastballs and so on are common. Among the basic pitches is the slider, a stepchild of a curve and a fastball. At its best, it can be a breaking pitch that gives hitters fits. Hang one, and it's fodder for a home run. And its origins appear to have beginnings with two pitchers who played in Cleveland.

Before we dive into Cleveland's ties to the origins of the pitch, here's a primer on the slider. There are differences between the throwing motions of a curveball and a slider. To throw a curve, a pitcher—right-handed, for instance—snaps his wrist sharply and downward, toward the plate. While there are variations, that snap usually occurs while the arm is above the pitcher's head near the middle of the motion. The ball will appear to be headed straight for a right-handed batter's head, and then, very suddenly, the ball will "break" across the plate. From a batter's or home-plate umpire's vantage, a sharp curveball actually will appear to jump, or hop, across the plate. A batter anticipating a curve tries to gauge the breaking moment and swing before the ball makes its leap. It's a gamble. A pitcher throwing a sharp curve might have an advantage. But if at the break the ball tends to "hang" or not jump sharply, the batter can tee off.

A slider differs in that the twist of the ball comes later in the motion. The overall motion resembles a fastball until that late twist.

Indians great Bob Feller breaks down pitches in his 1948 book, *Pitching to Win*. "It has become widely popular in recent years," he writes.

The slider behaves in a manner which its name implies. It breaks late and its course is much more horizontal than the curve ball. Hence, the name slider.

The grip is much different than for the fast ball and curve. It is held well off center to the outside. It does not spin as much as the curve ball and this adds to its deception. Batters often can guess that a ball will curve by detecting the spin of the ball, but they identify a slider as a fast ball until it is too late.

The delivery is almost identical with that of a fast ball until the point of release. I think the release can be best described by comparing it with the passing of a football. The index finger controls the release, even as it does a football, and the hand is about in the same position.

Unlike the curve, the snap of the wrist is late and the arm turns in only half as much as it does for the curve. To carry the metaphor further, the release of the slider is similar to the motion which would be used in pointing the index finger at home plate....

When the slider is fully developed it will break as much as five or six inches. It does not break as widely as a curve, but it can be more effective because of the suddenness of its action.

Feller goes on to say how much he relied on the curve in 1946, when he struck out a major-league best 348 batters. He also said the pitch can put "extra strain on elbow muscles."

The slider's origins, like many inventions or firsts, remain murky. The pitch appears to date to the late 1920s or early '30s. It evolved and gained in popularity.

(One name that occasionally surfaces as a possible creator of the pitch is Chief Bender, a Hall of Famer who played primarily with the Philadelphia Athletics. He won 212 games from 1903 to 1917. As Tom Swift writes in his SABR biography: "He threw a well-directed fastball and a sharp-breaking curve—a man named Bender has to have one—that was a precursor to the slider, a pitch he may have invented.... There is no one agreed-upon inventor of the slider.")

"The pitch of the 1960's was the slider. Virtually every pitcher at all levels of baseball added the pitch to their repertoire," a 2017 FoxSports report says. As a contemporary example, Randy Johnson is seen as having one of the best sliders ever. The six-foot, ten-inch Hall of Famer won 303 games.

But before Johnson or Steve Carlton or any other great who perfected the slider, there was a pair of Georges: George Uhle and George Blaeholder.

Left: Hall of Famer Randy Johnson had one of the best sliders around. *Curt Chandler, the Plain Dealer*.

Below: George Uhle and his wife, Ellen, in 1978. *Michael J. Zaremba, the Plain Dealer*.

The Cleveland-born Uhle grew up on the city's West Side off Lorain Avenue. When he was fifteen, players on one of his sandlot teams had to sell raffle tickets for uniforms. He stuck with it, moved up the semipro ranks and was referred to the Indians. He made his major-league debut in 1919.

Uhle played for four teams over seventeen seasons. One day, while he was with Detroit in 1929, Uhle warmed up, and a pitch was born. His Society for American Baseball Research biography states:

> *While pitching batting practice, with Tigers outfielder Harry Heilman [sic] in the cage, Uhle began to experiment with a new pitch. He released the baseball off his middle finger, much like a bowling ball. "What kind of a curve is that?" asked the Hall of Fame outfielder. "Hey, that's not a curve. That ball was sliding," replied Uhle. A new pitch called the slider was created, and George Uhle took full credit for it.*

Uhle corroborated that account to a reporter in 1978. "I named the slider while working with Harry Heilmann. He was catching it and it slithered, slid and jumped. Now they are breaking it too big. There are no sailing fastballs anymore."

In 1981, he repeated the story when a reporter talked to the former ballplayer, who was hospitalized at the time. Uhle referred again to pitching to Heilmann: "'I was experimenting. I held the ball this way.' He sat up in his hospital bed [and] demonstrated with his long fingers, holding an imaginary ball and releasing it off his middle finger similar to a bowling ball. Heilmann asked 'What kind of a curve is that?' I said 'Hey, that's not a curve. That ball was sliding.' And that's how it started."

And in *The Dickson Baseball Dictionary*, the story crops up again. "Harry Heilmann and I were just working (on the sidelines to catcher Eddie) Phillips. It just came to me all of a sudden, letting the ball go along my index finger and using my ring finger and pinky to give it just a little bit of a twist. It was a sailing fastball, and that's how come I named it the slider. The real slider is a sailing fastball."

And here is the case for Blaeholder. A 1936 newspaper report credits him as being a "master of a half-curve ball that is hard to hit." Steve O'Neill, his manager on the Indians that year, said, "He throws a 'slider' ball, that is, it looks like a fast ball, but breaks sharply and curves out. A right-handed batter fails to get it on the 'fat' of his bat, but hits it on the end of the stick.'"

His *Plain Dealer* obituary—Blaeholder died at age forty-three in 1947 of liver cancer—dealt almost exclusively with the slider. In a column headlined "Blaeholder Earns Place in Baseball History by Contributing Slider to Pitching Art," Gordon Cobbledick wrote: "It is doubted that Bob Feller could have broken the old strikeout record by Rube Waddell but for the pioneering Blaeholder did with the slider. Feller is perhaps the delivery's greatest master today. When mixed with his fast ball and curve it drives some of the most talented hitters to drink."

Several years later, Cobbledick revisited Blaeholder and the slider, digging a bit into history. "The slider was unheard of before 1928 because it didn't exist. This was the year a right-handed pitcher named George Blaeholder came up to the Texas League with a baffling new delivery. Batters used to go back to the bench after hitting against Blaeholder, muttering 'Every fast ball the guy throws is a curve.' Blaeholder was a big, good-natured Californian who had no wish to keep his secret. He taught the slider to other members of the Browns' staff, and trades and conversations soon spread it throughout the major leagues."

Blaeholder's SABR biography says *Baseball Digest* and the *Sporting News* credit him "as the inventor of the slider." The irony is that the bio on the back of a 1991 throwback baseball card showing Uhle's likeness includes this note: "George Uhle was one of the first pitchers to add the slider to his repertoire and coined the name 'slider.'" The card is from the *Sporting News* Conlon Collection.

The SABR biography, though, admits the difficulty in determining the slider's specific origin. "Uhle and Blaeholder called their pitches sliders and are generally considered the fathers of the pitch, which has certainly developed and morphed extensively since they used them."

Part of that development came in Cleveland in 1936.

That year, Uhle, Blaeholder and Feller all played for Cleveland. It was Feller's first season and Uhle's last. The two were born twenty years apart. In fact, Uhle was the only player on that team born in the nineteenth century. It also was Blaeholder's final year in the majors. Despite having played together, with ample time as they spent countless hours together on the sidelines, Feller in his book does not credit Blaeholder as the slider's inventor and does not mention Uhle in connection with the pitch at all. That's somewhat surprising, considering pitchers have their own fraternity and plenty of time to talk during games. Since there is documented research about Uhle and Blaeholder both throwing early sliders, it seems reasonable to envision

George Uhle is buried in Lakewood Park Cemetery in Rocky River. Uhle lays claim to having coined the term *slider*. *Marc Bona.*

the two veterans bookending the seventeen-year-old Feller on the bench and offering pitching advice.

"The late George Blaeholder is generally credited with the development of the pitch in the early thirties, but I cannot testify to the truth of this," Feller writes.

A story by ESPN's Rob Neyer summarizes the slider's genesis this way: "There is no Eureka! moment for the slider, in large part because nobody really knows when, or even approximately when, the first slider was thrown....The slider is generally attributed to one of two Georges (if not both)...Blaeholder, and Uhle."

Whether it was Uhle or Blaeholder, it appears there's a good chance that the father of the slider was a pitcher who at one time wore an Indian jersey.

17

THE LONGEST GAME

The Cleveland Barons had the best record in the International-American Hockey League in 1937–38. They received a bye in the playoffs. But a series of injuries depleted the team to only ten players when they hosted the Syracuse Stars in a must-win playoff game on April 4, 1938.

Almost every seat was filled in the ten-thousand-seat Cleveland Arena on Euclid Avenue when the teams met for Game 2 in the best-of-three series. The Stars had captured the opener, 6–3, in Syracuse the night before.

Cleveland had finished with the league's best record, atop the three-team Western Division at 25-12-11. Going into the playoffs, the Barons had lost only one of sixteen overtime games that season. They were almost perfect at home, losing only once.

Syracuse had finished third in the Western Division and had to beat second-place Pittsburgh to advance to play Cleveland. Even though Cleveland had a bye, Syracuse had home-ice advantage because the Toronto Ice Carnival was already booked at the arena. The Barons also had to contend with the Stars' Jack Markle and Eddie Convey, the league's top scorers and the only two players to tally more than fifty points in the forty-eight-game season.

Even the Barons' thirty-eight-year-old player-coach Bill Cook said Cleveland's winning the title would be "remarkable."

Here's the litany of injuries the Barons suffered: Earl Bartholome came down with appendicitis in March; Bud Cook broke his leg; Art Berlett was out because of a bad back; and Peg O'Neill had blood poisoning. But the most seriously injured player was Earl Roche, who in the final period of the opener at Syracuse was hit in the right eye by a teammate's stick and had to be rushed to the hospital. Doctors were preparing Roche for surgery but decided to wait to see if his hemorrhage would subside. He was diagnosed with a contusion and remained in the hospital. That meant that, going into Game 2, the Barons were down to eleven players. But when Max Bennett checked Oscar Hanson hard in the first period, Hanson had to be carried off the ice with a leg injury, and the team was pared to ten. (Compare that to the more than two dozen players on an NHL team roster nowadays.) Hanson was the sixth player the team had lost since they filed their eligibility list on February 28 for the playoffs.

Despite that, Phil Hergesheimer banged in the puck from a scrum in front of the net in the first period to give Cleveland a 1–0 lead. Syracuse came back when Bill Thompson fired a shot from the right point to tie the game at 1–1. Cleveland took the lead again when Les Cunningham beat two defenders and scored, making it 2–1 going into the third. But Thompson scored again for Syracuse, and the game went to overtime.

Overtime rules called for a ten-minute, non-sudden-death period, followed by subsequent sudden-death twenty-minute periods if necessary. The teams battled and slogged through OT, the Barons trying desperately to keep up without fresh legs. They even had to play short-handed after they incurred two penalties. Finally, after twelve minutes and forty-two seconds of the fourth overtime, Max Bennett beat Barons goaltender Moe Roberts with a thirty-foot shot, giving Syracuse a 3–2 win and eliminating the Barons. The game ended at 1:15 a.m.

John Dietrich's lead in the *Plain Dealer* the following day dramatically summed up the game: "Ten men against fifteen, ten men in a daze of fatigue, staggering to the finish of the longest professional hockey game on record here, Cleveland's valiant Barons last night finally went down and out in the International-American League race."

It stood as the longest overtime game in AHL history until 1982. The 1938 game remains the fifth-longest AHL overtime game. (The leagues merged soon after the 1938 season, and the 'International' was dropped in 1940.)

The game is left as a footnote in hockey history, but it has an odd, indirect connection to one of the most memorable sports movies, *Slap Shot*.

The Barons' Oscar Hanson (the original spelling was Hansen, but it alternated in accounts over the years) hailed from a large hockey-playing family, with several of the brothers often playing on the same teams together. In all, there were ten Hansons, seven boys and three girls. Emery Hanson also played for the Barons in 1937–38.

Oscar played eleven years, all in the minors save for eight games of the 1937–38 season in the NHL with Chicago. In 1934, three of the brothers—Emery, Oscar and Emil—played for the St. Paul Saints, the only trio of brothers competing on the same professional hockey team.

Five Hansons—Julius, Joe, Louis, Emil and Oscar—had played for Augsburg College in Minneapolis. The team had been selected to represent the United States at the 1928 Olympics, which was set to be held in St. Moritz, Switzerland. But the offer was rescinded by Major General Douglas MacArthur, chairman of the U.S. Olympic committee. The team, not long before it was to travel to the Games, had been deemed not sufficiently "representative."

The Hansons played into the 1940s.

Fast-forward three decades, and the story alternates between art and life. In *Slap Shot*, Reggie Dunlop, played by Paul Newman, tries to hold his rough-and-tumble Charlestown Chiefs together in a depressed mill town. The Chiefs feature a trio of brothers known as the Hansons who were always willing to drop the gloves with opponents. Brothers Jeff and Steve Carlson played two of the Hansons, with Dave Hanson playing Jack Hanson. (Dave Hanson is not related to the Hansons who played for Cleveland.)

Oscar Hanson, who was injured early in the overtime game, had a son named Jerry who had played hockey when he was young. But Hansen—Jerry has the "e" in his name—was also into auto racing and owned Brainerd International Raceway, about 130 miles north of Minneapolis–St. Paul. He became friends with Newman, a racing aficionado. When Newman visited the track, he sometimes stayed at Hansen's home and spent time with his family. Newman even set a lap record on the track in 1977 and won races there.

But the Hanson name for the hockey-playing brothers in the movie does not stem from the brothers who played for Cleveland, according to Jonathon Jackson, who wrote *The Making of Slap Shot* in 2010.

Almost forty years earlier, though, the real Hanson brothers weren't thinking movies. They were all about hockey. A day after the marathon game, the Barons split a $5,000 bonus at a gala held at Canterbury Country Club in the village of Beachwood. That bonus would be worth more than $90,000 today.

Syracuse would go on to lose to Providence in the finals.

Hergesheimer, who scored the game's first goal, twice led the AHL in goals, scoring twenty-five in 1937–38 and thirty-four in the 1938–39 season. That year, Cleveland won the championship, the first of the Barons' nine league titles.

Bennett, who scored the winning goal for Syracuse, had played one game in the National Hockey League for Montreal in the 1935–36 season and then spent the next nine seasons in the minors, never to return to the NHL.

Slap Shot continues to hold its cult-like sports-film status more than forty years after its release. In 2020, the *Chicago Tribune* ranked it as the eighth-best sports film of all time. *Rolling Stone* tabbed it the seventh best in 2015. And Bleacher Report has it at number ten.

It also has a fun tie to Cleveland's current AHL team, the Monsters. For several seasons, the "Mullet brothers"—a trio of glasses-wearing skaters resembling the Hanson brothers from the movie—scooped up ice shavings between time stoppages and, with (faux) stern looks, slammed the glass to the delight of onlooking young fans. In 2014, Christian Hanson, who alternated between the AHL and NHL over six seasons, had tried out for the Monsters but was cut in training camp. He is the son of hockey-playing dad Dave, who played Jack Hanson in the movie.

The Cleveland Barons remained in the American Hockey League until 1973. The Cleveland Arena, the team's early home, was demolished in April 1977, the year *Slap Shot* was released.

18

A Sporting Life

Billy Evans was one of the most integral people to play a part in baseball without having been a professional player, coach or manager. He was a pioneer, a boy wonder who evolved and moved from one aspect of the game to the next over almost half a century, much of it spent in Cleveland.

An early moment in Evans's career helped shape who he became. Evans was born in 1884 and grew up in Youngstown, graduating from the Rayen School. He was an athlete, a 175-pound halfback on the football team that won a championship. He attended Cornell University, playing football (halfback) and baseball (outfielder). His coach was Hughie Jennings, who, like Evans, would wind up in the Baseball Hall of Fame years later. Jennings said that Evans would have been a "promising" major leaguer, but a dislocated knee suffered in football derailed his career as a player.

He returned home during his junior year when his father died, landing a job at the *Youngstown Vindicator* as a sportswriter, making fifteen dollars a week. He was covering a game between Youngstown Ohio Works and a team from Homestead, Pennsylvania, in 1903, when he was drafted to fill in for an ill umpire. Managers had conferred, then approached Evans. He recounted the story in a column years later.

> *It's funny to me now as I look back on that game. I felt like the original fish out of water. There I was, Billy Evans, a young sports writer dragged*

from the grandstand to umpire a game against my will. And all the time it was Old Man Opportunity knocking at the back door. My attitude toward umpiring was much as the average small boy's of today. There was something alluring enough about being a ball player, but who in thunder entertained any ambitions of becoming an umpire?

He wound up doing "such a bangup job that he was hired as a regular." With that came a huge increase in pay. He was offered fifteen dollars a game and, for a while, kept his sportswriting gig.

It was a time when an umpire's job was tough, thankless and solitary (one umpire per game). After a game in Pennsylvania in 1906, a reported crowd of several hundred, no doubt displeased with Evans's calls, followed him to his hotel, though they scattered when they thought he had a gun. It turned out to be a whistle, and Evans, ever the diplomat, managed to calm them and even invited some back to his hotel.

Evans came of age one day in 1905 on a ball field in Ohio during a game between Youngstown and Niles, in a story that would be recounted at different times over the years. It was filled with that dramatic moment of truth that comes every so often: ninth inning, bases loaded, two out, full count. Youngstown was ahead by a run. The pitch came in, and the Niles batter fell as if he had avoided a wild pitch and trotted to first. Evans called a strike. Game over. Evans had to be escorted out of the park—and the city, reportedly. In one of the greatest understatements, a writer years later recounting the incident wrote, "that decision was unpopular with Niles fans." To say the least.

The young umpire didn't know it, but in the stands sat St. Louis Brown manager Jim McAleer, who was scouting a player. McAleer was so impressed by Evans's steadfastness that he recommended him to American League president Ban Johnson. The rest, as they say, is history. That year, Evans was named an American League umpire. He was twenty-two, the youngest person to this day to become a major-league umpire. He had made an extraordinary leap from low-level minors to the majors. (McAleer and Evans had attended the same high school, years apart.)

Evans took to officiating immediately. In 1905, the eight-team American League had only five umpires. He also became known in the "roller polo" circuit. The sport, mainly floor hockey on roller skates, was popular at the time.

When he was called up, he was described as one of the best umpires in Ohio. He settled in, and his first-year assessment was "very good."

During his second year, though, things got a little rough—literally. The 1907 season saw Evans work seven doubleheaders alone in eight days. But the low point came late in the season, when a teenage fan threw a soda bottle that hit Evans in the head. He suffered a fractured skull and was knocked unconscious. While he recuperated, reports speculated that Evans might quit. Hearing that the teen was contrite about the incident, Evans did not press charges. National League president Harry Pulliam put forth a proposal to ban the sale of bottles. One end-of-year account, lauding Evans's umpiring, flippantly noted, "He is a topnotch official and the only referee, umpire or arbiter in the business who can bounce pop bottles off his head one week and officiate the next."

Jim McAleer and Billy Evans attended the same high school, Rayen, in Youngstown, about twenty years apart. *Benjamin K. Edwards Collection via Library of Congress.*

Two years after the bottle incident, Evans found himself in his first World Series, again the youngest umpire ever, at age twenty-five. Pittsburgh and Detroit faced off with two of the game's luminaries, Honus Wagner and Ty Cobb, respectively, gracing the field. Detroit was managed by Hughie Jennings, Evans's college baseball coach. Evans umpired in six World Series, including the infamous 1919 Black Sox matchup between the Cincinnati Reds and the Chicago White Sox.

"He substituted diplomacy for belligerency and proved an arbiter could control a game without threats of physical violence," a newspaper writer penned years later. "But unlike some umpires, Billy Evans never pretended to be infallible. 'I missed a lot of decisions during my…years as an umpire. At the time of making such a decision there was no doubt in my mind as to its correctness. However, a second or two later I felt that I erred and wished I could change my original ruling.'"

His brand of diplomacy, though, had its limits. The fiery Cobb once challenged him to a postgame fight, which Evans accepted. Both men, in their thirties, slugged it out before a crowd under the stands. By multiple accounts, Evans gave as good as he got, and the two ended up shaking hands.

Evans was among the umpires who "showed something new" by running down the first-base line to follow a play. He also urged the creation of a formal umpiring school, which exists today.

Evans never forgot his writing roots, though. He was the sports editor of the Newspaper Enterprise Association, a syndicate, for most of the 1920s, writing a weekly column called "Billy Evans Says." Hundreds of clients subscribed. He was signed to cover the 1920 World Series. He authored two books, *Umpiring from the Inside* in 1947 and *Knotty Problems in Baseball* in 1950.

"No umpire," he writes in his 1947 book, "is infallible." He goes on to say that star players gripe less than mediocre ones, that the latter occasionally "seeks to cover up lack of natural talent by resorting to alibis at the expense of the umpire."

Evans offers keys to success he gleaned from his more than two decades umpiring. "I am firmly convinced that a willingness to listen to any reasonable protest was one of my greatest assets in keeping out of trouble." He adds that those keys are formed by the combined qualities of "good eyesight, despite the accepted theory of fandom that all umpires are blind….plenty of common sense, a dash of diplomacy here and there, strict discipline at the proper spot, confidence in his ability, a show of aggressiveness in order to be convincing, and last, but not least, a thorough knowledge of the playing rules."

He "thought up trick situations" and would write about them, kind of an early version of former *Plain Dealer* sports editor Hal Lebovitz's well-known "Ask Hal the Referee" column. He offered an inside-the-sport vantage, a rare peek at an umpire's take on rules. Balks, for instance, were one of the most difficult calls to make. He also offered his opinion of certain ballplayers, an amazing and unheard-of thing nowadays.

In 1911, Evans penned a thoughtful piece on players, giving a glimpse of them as people, writing that all fans see are well-paid stars with the trappings of life handed to them, while the other, hidden side holds the odds they have overcome, the life on the road, the work and countless hours of preparation they put in.

Despite his solid standing through his years as an arbiter in the sport, Evans—late one night and over drinks, long after he had left umpiring—confided to a columnist that he had stayed too long as an umpire. He had been upset about critical comments from the columnist, Lyall Smith, but calmed down, and they chatted. Smith kept the comments off the record until after Evans died.

In twenty-two years, Evans umpired 3,319 games. He was on the field for four no-hitters.

Billy Evans as a young umpire, and his crypt frontispiece at Knollwood Cemetery in Mayfield Heights, Ohio. *Author collection.*

He left umpiring in 1927 for the rare leap into the front office, becoming general manager for the Indians when the term *GM* wasn't used often. He found players like Joe Vosmik, Earl Averill and Wes Ferrell.

Just as he was the youngest umpire when he broke into the majors, he was the youngest general manager. He was forty-three.

In 1928, he hired Roger Peckinpaugh, who guided the Tribe to just over .500 in his initial five-plus seasons with the club. Evans was one of the people responsible for lowering the League Park screen by ten feet in the stadium's notoriously short right field. He pushed for the team's spring-training home to be moved from New Orleans to California to be in better proximity to more clubs, prescient thinking considering the geographic clusters teams now use. He expanded Ladies Day to a regular home-Friday promotion in 1934.

But Evans wasn't always on the cutting edge. Before the 1935 season, he came out opposed to night baseball. In fairness to Evans, his logic was sound: He saw more competition for baseball at night from "theaters, parties, dine-and-dance spots, outdoor amusement parks and a long list of other entertainment facilities," as one writer summed up Evans's position. "We've got enough competition now without looking for more," Evans was quoted as saying. On May 24, Cincinnati hosted Philadelphia in the first night game in the majors, and the sport was forever changed.

Differences with owner Alva Bradley highlighted by a steep pay cut led to Evans leaving for Boston to head the Red Sox farm system. Evans's pay had topped out at $30,000 during his time as the Indians' general manager, but it had been cut over time to $7,500. (To compare, according to 2010 figures, most general managers were pulling in between $500,000 and $2 million.) His $7,500 salary would equate to six figures today.

He spent several years as Boston's chief scout but left because of a rift with player-manager Joe Cronin. Evans had found a talented shortstop—Cronin's position—with Louisville. Cronin saw otherwise, and owner Tom Yawkey traded the young shortstop to Brooklyn. The promising shortstop was Pee Wee Reese, who would play sixteen years in the big leagues and wind up in the Hall of Fame.

After his time in the front office for Cleveland followed by his battles with Cronin, it seems Evans had soured on the game he loved. He left baseball for what turned out to be a one-year sabbatical but returned to Cleveland to become general manager of the Cleveland Rams football team. He became the first man to hold top front-office jobs in "bigtime" football and baseball.

As he did in his umpiring and baseball general-manager days, Evans took an innovative approach to his job. He had the field at Cleveland Municipal Stadium shifted to be parallel to the third-base line for fans to have a better vantage. He was making $15,000 in his role with the Rams, which included scouting, publicity and promotion in addition to his GM duties.

He saw fit to create camaraderie on the team, once buying forty tickets to take his players to boxing matches at Cleveland Arena.

In his sole season with the Rams, one player Evans signed eventually would have a lasting impact on the game. Red Hickey would play five years for the Rams and later become a coach. As a coach in 1960, he pioneered the shotgun formation—rare then but common in today's passing attack.

Evans also believed that baseball should take after football when it came to rules regarding the signing of college players. Football at the time did not negotiate with undergraduates, a stance he wanted baseball to take as well to avoid college players being stolen before their eligibility was finished. Whether Evans would have changed his thinking on this topic remains speculation. While all major sports leagues have age requirements, they can draft and sign players long before college eligibility is up.

But despite a restrained optimistic outlook he presented at the beginning of the season in the press, Evans could only do so much, and the team sank to the cellar, finishing 2-9. And Evans found himself pulled back into his first love, baseball.

He was named president of the Southern Association in 1942, which required that he muster every bit of the acumen he had gained over the

Billy Evans's final resting place is in this mausoleum in Knollwood Cemetery in Mayfield Heights, Ohio. At some point, someone placed a baseball on the ledge, which is about ten feet off the ground. *Marc Bona.*

years, considering leagues struggled during the trying times of World War II. Not only did the league survive under Evans's leadership, but it also made money—no small accomplishment.

He returned to the major leagues in what would be his swan song, as executive vice-president and general manager of the Detroit Tigers (1946–52), and then he retired.

Evans died in 1956 after a stroke. Former athletes and others poured out tributes. He was known as a "dapper dresser," "devout Presbyterian" and family man, as his Society for American Baseball Research biography notes. He is buried in Knollwood Cemetery in Mayfield Heights.

Evans was elected to the Baseball Hall of Fame in 1973, the third umpire enshrined.

Billy Evans enjoyed a long life in baseball covering the first half of the twentieth century, seamlessly moving from one aspect of the game to another.

His obituary in the *Plain Dealer* sums up his life: "William George (Billy) Evans never played a lick of professional baseball, yet became one of the sport's leading figures."

19

A Forgotten Dynasty

E ach sport has its dynasties—by team, by decade. In football, we have the Green Bay Packers under Vince Lombardi in the 1960s, the Pittsburgh Steelers and their balanced offensive and defensive play in the 1970s, on to the San Francisco 49ers a decade later and, in recent years, the New England Patriots.

But the one that stays tucked away in history is the Cleveland Browns. From 1946 to 1949, the Browns dominated the All-America Football Conference, a rival to the NFL. The AAFC lasted four years and merged with the NFL beginning with the 1950 season.

How good were the Browns? They won all the league championships, compiling a four-year record of 47-4-3. Choose any NFL team's stretch over four straight seasons from 1950 to the present day and you would be hard-pressed to find one that tops Cleveland's 87 percent winning record. They shut out opponents eight times on their way to winning four championships. Their season records and title game results are as follows:

1946   *12-2, beat New York Yankees, 14–9, in Cleveland.*
1947   *12-1-1, beat New York Yankees, 14–3, in New York.*
1948   *14-0, beat Buffalo Bills, 49–7, in Cleveland.*
1949   *9-1-2, beat San Francisco 49ers, 21–7, in Cleveland.*

The 1940s team was led by Paul Brown, the pioneering coach whose innovative marks on football remain to this day, from playbooks to scouting and much more.

Cleveland Brown coach Paul Brown (*center*) accepts an original painting that appeared on a *Sports Illustrated* cover. He is shown with William B. Clark (*left*), a Cleveland representative of the magazine, and Clem Young, president of the Touchdown Club. *Richard J. Misch, the Plain Dealer.*

The league was founded on June 4, 1944, its roots planted forty-eight hours before Allied troops stormed the beaches of Normandy and World War II turned the corner toward its finish. Eight teams began play in the league two years later. Under Brown, his teams rolled. No fewer than seven players wound up in the Hall of Fame, including famed quarterback Otto Graham, kicker Lou "The Toe" Groza, Hudson-born Dante Lavelli and the league's first two Black players, lineman Bill Willis and fullback Marion Motley. (The two broke into the professional ranks in September 1946, seven months before Jackie Robinson made his Major League Baseball debut, ending the color barrier that had been in place for decades.)

Over the AAFC's four-year existence, Cleveland lost four games, two each to the San Francisco 49ers and Los Angeles Dons. They tied Buffalo twice, in the same season (1949). They lost only two home games in four years, to San Francisco in 1946 and to Los Angeles in 1947. In 1946, they lost back-to-back games, the only time Cleveland lost consecutive contests in the 1940s.

The Browns began by winning seven games, outscoring opponents 180–34. Then, on October 27, 1946, they faced San Francisco at home. The day resulted in bad things all around for Cleveland: A wild play, a winning streak broken, an injury and a tragedy averted.

A wacky play in the first quarter seemed to indicate that the bounces were going San Francisco's way. The 49ers' Frankie Albert punted to Graham, who fumbled on the runback. Two San Francisco players picked it up and fumbled before it was recovered—by Albert. It set up the 49ers' touchdown. In the second quarter, the Browns' Cliff Lee (who had gone to Lakewood High School) was "smothered" by a San Francisco lineman and twisted his knee. He was taken to Charity Hospital. General Jonathan M. Wainwright, a decorated war hero, attended the game and was honored at halftime. When the gun sounded, the Browns had lost, 34–20. It was the most points any Browns team would let up in a game in their first three seasons. Meanwhile, on the East Side of Cleveland on the morning of the game, a seventeen-year-old saved his father and younger brother as a fire ravaged the family home. His heroics dominated the *Plain Dealer*'s coverage on page one.

A week later, the Browns traveled to Los Angeles to play the Dons. Lou Groza, who was injured in several games and playing with a bad back, missed a point-after attempt. A field goal with eighteen seconds remaining gave the Dons a one-point win. They would be the only losses for the Browns that season, but there would be one obstacle remaining for them to overcome before the championship game on December 22 between New York and Cleveland.

On December 14, several Cleveland players sat in a car behind a police officer, waiting to pick up a teammate's wife. Inebriated and impatient, they honked and yelled, "Do the police own the road?" Lou Rymkus, Mac Speedie and tackle Jim Daniell were arrested. Who among the players instigated the confrontation remains unclear. The case would be thrown out the day after the championship game. But Paul Brown doled out different punishments. As captain, Daniell was supposed to act in a more responsible manner and was held to a higher standard. A decorated World War II veteran who had played at Ohio State, Daniell was fined and kicked off the team. He never played again. His teammates, though, awarded him a full share of the title game proceeds, which amounted to $931.57.

In the 1946 championship, Harvey Johnson (who would later go on to coach O.J. Simpson and the Buffalo Bills) booted a chip-shot field goal from the 11-yard line, giving the Yankees a 3–0 lead early in the first quarter. The Browns erased the deficit when Marion Motley plunged through from the 1-yard line before halftime. The Yankees scored a touchdown on a two-yard run by

Spec Sanders in the third quarter, giving them a 9–7 lead. But Graham hit Lavelli for a sixteen-yard touchdown for the go-ahead score with four minutes, thirty-one seconds remaining on a cold afternoon that saw the mercury barely nudge above freezing. From that point, the Browns were never behind in a championship game, including 1964. Cleveland-born Governor Thomas J. Herbert said over a loudspeaker, "A rugged day and a rugged game."

In 1947, the Browns rolled through their first five games. Then they hosted the Los Angeles Dons on October 12. At halftime, the Browns led, 10–7. Los Angeles tied the game on a forty-six-yard field goal in the third quarter from Ben Agajanian. With the score tied and less than three minutes remaining in the game, the Dons recovered a Cleveland fumble, the Browns' third of the day. It set up Agajanian from the 28-yard line. His kick went wide, and it appeared there would be life left for the Browns to come back in the final minutes. But a flag was thrown on the play. Cleveland was penalized for having twelve men on the field, not a common foul. The ball was moved up five yards, and this time, Agajanian hit it for the go-ahead score.

But here's the kicker to the story, so to speak: Agajanian was missing four toes on his right foot, the result of an accident that took place six years earlier while he was working in a bottling plant. He wore a squared-off shoe and was known as "Bootin' Ben the Toeless Wonder." He died at age ninety-eight in 2018. In a connected twist of fate, the same year he hit the field goal, 1947, a man named Tom Dempsey was born without toes on his right foot. He became a kicker and, in 1970, booted a sixty-three-yard game-winning field goal for the New Orleans Saints over the Detroit Lions. That record stood until 2013, when Denver's Matt Prater kicked a sixty-four-yard field goal.

A footnote to the story is that Dempsey topped the previous record of fifty-six yards set by Bert Rechichar in 1953 for the Baltimore Colts. Unlike Agajanian and Dempsey, Rechichar, a defensive back, wasn't missing any toes, but it was his first-ever attempt at kicking a field goal. He holds a rare distinction. In 1952, he was a member of the Cleveland Browns and also played in the Indians' minor-league organization.

On November 2, 1947, the Browns traveled to Buffalo. From the Cleveland 1-yard line, Graham found Mac Speedie on a screen pass. Speedie, who was leading the league in receiving, made a move on a defender to get open. He took the pass and, with three teammates protecting him, raced downfield, saw one defender closing in and turned on the jets. The result was a ninety-nine-yard touchdown. The NFL has recorded thirteen ninety-nine-yard touchdown passes. As of this writing, Graham-to-Speedie is the only connection of that distance between two Hall of Famers.

The only other blemish on the Browns' record in 1947 was a tie on November 23 at Yankee Stadium. The Browns had to come back from a 28–0 deficit, a newspaper account calling the Browns a "bewildered, disorganized eleven" for the first half. But Cleveland responded on the strength of Graham's poise before more than seventy thousand fans, the largest crowd to see a football game in New York. Graham finished with 325 yards in the air while Lou Saban filled in for an ailing Groza, who had pulled a leg muscle. Spec Sanders accounted for 147 of New York's 269 yards on the ground. (The Browns would return to New York a few weeks later in a rematch for the championship, which they won, 14–3.)

The schedule had the Browns playing two games in five days as they traveled to Los Angeles to play the Dons on Thanksgiving. Cleveland avenged its sole loss of the season, winning 27–17.

A look at the Browns' dominance in the 1940s isn't complete without a mention of the draw play. That ubiquitous play, in which a quarterback appears to fade to pass before suddenly handing off, has become a staple in offenses (though, in recent years, it has showed a slight decline in use). Graham accidentally invented the play. This is what happened during one game, according to Duey Graham, Otto's son:

> A pass play was called and at the snap the center stepped back early onto Otto's planted foot. In the process of dropping back, Otto's balance was thrown off causing him to stumble while trying to gather his balance. As he continued back, realizing he couldn't recover, Otto saw Marion Motley in his protection block position and stuffed the ball into his fullback's stomach as he stumbled by. Marion stood there dumbfounded covering the ball as the defensive rushers passed him by to pile onto the fallen quarterback. (In those days, a player had to be held down for the play to be over). Once the rush passed him by, Motley took off for a substantial gain. On the sideline, Paul Brown watched the botched play and instantly recognized its potential. At the next practice, there were four "draw" plays on the chalkboard.

Years later, Paul Brown admitted that the inaugural play was an accident but said, "We decided we had something good and we put it in our playbook as a regular formation." As Otto Graham once said, "All Paul's inventions were based on his reaction to needs."

The Browns were perfect in 1948. They averaged over twenty-nine points while allowing fourteen per game. On November 25, the Browns played their first of two games within four days on the West Coast. On Thanksgiving, they beat Los Angeles, 31–14, while Graham suffered what was initially thought to be a serious knee injury. A game-time decision on November 28, Brown let Graham decide whether to play. He did, throwing four touchdowns, and the Browns clinched a title game berth. Writers lauded the Browns as "the greatest football team ever assembled." Several weeks later, they easily beat the Bills for their third consecutive championship.

In recent years, the streak that stands in the minds of Browns' fans is the nineteen consecutive games the team went without a win until September 20, 2018. But within their four-year span in the AAFC, the Browns compiled an impressive twenty-seven-game regular-season unbeaten streak. On October 19, 1947, they beat the Chicago Rockets. They did not lose again until October 9, 1949, when the San Francisco 49ers handed the Browns a 56–28 thrashing.

That season, the AAFC instituted playoffs. Previously, the two division leaders met for the title. But this year, a four-team playoff was put in place. Cleveland met Buffalo in a semifinal match, winning 31–21. It was the third time the teams had met in 1949, the first two ending in ties. The Browns met their Western Division foes, the 49ers, for the title in Cleveland and won, 21–7. Both games were in Cleveland.

When the players suited up for the 1949 title game, they knew the league had merged with the NFL. That announcement came two days prior to the game. The merger agreement included Cleveland, Baltimore and San Francisco joining the rival "National League," while the others folded or merged. Los Angeles, which in 1949 had two AAFC teams, for instance, meshed into one in the National League.

One report summed it up this way: "The new league amounts to a victory for the National League and a surrender for the All America Conference. The AAC had wanted to retain its identity as a separate league; the National League last year proposed that it take Cleveland and San Francisco into its fold and eliminate all other AAC teams."

Once they got to the NFL, the Browns continued their stellar play. Their first six years in the league, they played in the championship game, winning three times. In fact, for a thirty-year span, from the moment they began play in 1950 until 1980, the Browns had only four losing seasons.

Cleveland sports fans are well aware that the Cavaliers' championship in 2016 broke the fifty-two-year drought without a major-sport team title, the Browns having won in 1964. But the 1946–49 Browns proved they were definitely not a one-hit wonder with their dominance before the NFL gained in popularity.

20

POTATO BALL

In a late-season minor-league game in 1987, a catcher with the Williamsport Bills, a Class AA affiliate of the Cleveland Indians, decided to have some fun. Dave Bresnahan secretly carved a potato into a baseball, hid it in his mitt and, at the right moment, threw it past third base, enticing a runner to race home. He tagged the runner with the real baseball. It was the old hidden-ball trick. The umpire didn't think it was funny. Bresnahan's manager thought it even less funny. And a once-promising ballplayer in the Indians' organization saw his career end.

Bresnahan wasn't born in Ohio, but he has ties to one of the game's pioneers who was. His great-uncle, Hall-of-Fame catcher Roger Bresnahan, is credited with inventing shin guards. He wore them on Opening Day in 1907 with the New York Giants. Roger Bresnahan was born, raised and died in Toledo. He even bought the Toledo Mud Hens at one point.

Dave Bresnahan was raised in the Chicago suburbs but moved to Arizona at a young age. When Bresnahan broke his throwing hand, he taught himself to throw left-handed. He was a switch-hitting catcher, an attractive quality to prospective teams. The Seattle Mariners selected him in the eighteenth round of the 1984 draft, which saw the likes of Cory Snyder go fourth overall to Cleveland, Mark McGwire tenth to Oakland, Greg Maddux thirty-first to the Chicago Cubs and Tom Glavine forty-seventh to Atlanta. Bresnahan—one of three players selected in that draft from Grand Canyon University—began his professional career with Bellingham in the Northwest League before playing for Wausau in the Midwest League. The Indians picked him up, and he joined Waterloo, also in the Midwest

League, in 1986. The following season, he was sent up to Class AA Williamsport in the Eastern League.

The Bills, tucked in north-central Pennsylvania, spent only two seasons as an Indians' affiliate (former Indian player and coach Mike Hargrove was their final manager in 1988), and the team simply wasn't that good. In 1987, Bresnahan's sole year with the Bills, the team finished 60-79, 27.5 games out of first place. Nine players on the '87 team would make it to the majors, including Rod Nichols, who played five of his seven big-league seasons with the Indians. One of the players was two-sport star Turner Gill, who had played quarterback at the University of Nebraska. The following year, the Bills improved to 66-73, 15 games behind.

Dave Bresnahan of the Williamsport Bills. *Courtesy of Williamsport Crosscutters.*

Bresnahan, a twenty-five-year-old backup catcher whose résumé that season included a brief demotion to Class A, was dragging a .150 average into the final games. He had spent nine games with Kinston but was sent back to Class AA in the domino effect created when Indian catcher Rick Dempsey was injured in a collision with Bo Jackson and another catcher was moved up. As the season wore on, losses mounting in the Pennsylvania summer, Bresnahan and his roommate, Rob Swain, were at a local pub. Sports shows were airing on a television, showing highlights of a game on August 3, 1987, when Minnesota pitcher Joe Niekro was ejected for using an emery board to scuff pitches. The home-plate umpire had called time to inspect the baseball. In the now-infamous moment, Niekro, surrounded by umpires and teammates at the mound, cleans out his pockets and tries to surreptitiously toss the emery board aside. But he is spotted by an umpire.

Bresnahan had remembered a story years earlier about a player who had introduced a potato into a game. That recollection, coupled with his team miles out of contention and the season basically over, spawned Bresnahan's idea to try to pull the hidden-ball trick using a potato. The joke would go like this: Bresnahan would throw to third to try to pick off a runner, but he would heave the potato instead of the baseball. When the player came home, the catcher would tag the runner with the real ball.

Bresnahan planned the caper carefully. He went to Weis Market and bought a bag of taters, even telling a clerk that his parents were coming to town as an excuse for the purchase. He borrowed a peeler (what minor-league ballplayer would have a potato peeler?) and scraped, then whittled, until he had one that looked something like a baseball. A baseball, it should be noted, weighs about five ounces, while a typical baking potato tips the Toledos around fourteen ounces. But once you peel and carve it into a sphere, a potato and a baseball will be comparable in weight.

"It's a slippery bastard when you try to throw it," Bresnahan told a reporter years later.

In his preparation for the joke, Bresnahan and teammates considered the rules: What would happen? One of Bresnahan's teammates asked his friend Tim Tschida, a young major-league umpire, who told him that he would just send the runner back to third. Tschida, by the way, was the home-plate umpire who suspected Niekro of doctoring the ball in the major-league game weeks earlier.

But the prank couldn't be pulled off without the blessings of his teammates. One was reluctant: pitcher Mike Poehl. A first-round selection of the Indians in 1985, Poehl was hesitant to join the prank because the play would have an adverse effect on his statistics.

Bresnahan chose August 31 to pull off the joke. It was a doubleheader against Reading, so he knew he would play one of the games. He also knew fans would turn out, as the Phillie Phanatic was coming in as a promotion; 3,258 fans showed up. All he needed was a runner on third base. And in the fifth inning, with Reading catcher Rick Lundblade on third with two out, the joke was set up. Bresnahan called time and told home-plate umpire Scott Potter the webbing was busted and he needed a new mitt. He ran back to the dugout to get the replacement mitt, which had the potato tucked in the webbing, a ready accomplice as teammates stifled giggles. As luck would have it, Poehl was on the mound for the Bills but had reluctantly agreed to play along. Bresnahan deftly held the potato in his right hand as he called for a low-and-away slider, and Poehl delivered. Bresnahan wheeled and threw to Swain at third base, deliberately throwing a bit wild. Bresnahan tossed his mask and cursed as Lundblade broke for home. And that's when Bresnahan tagged him with the real ball.

A potato is heavier than a baseball, but once you carve the vegetable into a sphere, they are closer in weight. *Marc Bona*.

"Hey Rick, you're out," he said as his counterpart reached the plate. It was a hidden-ball trick with a twist.

Left-fielder Miguel Roman—not in on the joke—ran over to pick up what he thought was the ball past third base and was perplexed. The third-base coach saw it and started screaming. Reading manager George Culver—who had played his first two seasons in the majors in 1966 and 1967 with the Indians—ran onto the field. Players pleaded with Potter, but he wasn't having any of it. Thinking the players were showing him up, he allowed the run to count. He did not eject Bresnahan, but the player's career was about to end.

Williamsport manager Orlando Gomez, a serious baseball guy by all accounts, didn't like the joke. When the Bills came off the field after the third out, he told Bresnahan to take off his catching gear. An inning later, Gill's two-run single turned out to be the difference in the game, and Williamsport won, 4–3. Poehl went the distance. (Reading won the nightcap to gain the split.)

Gomez was having none of the joke. He called the Indians' front office between games and wanted to release Bresnahan right then. Jeff Scott, the team's director of player development, took the more rational route and told the manager he didn't want to be left without a backup catcher for the second game. Scott, who liked Bresnahan, wasn't as angry as Gomez, but the team released the catcher. Gomez added insult to injury by fining the now–lame duck Bresnahan.

"I fined him $50. It was an unthinkable act for a professional," Gomez was quoted in a newspaper account the following day.

So it was back to Weis Market, where Bresnahan bought another sack of spuds. He left one in each of his teammates' lockers and put the remainder on Gomez's desk with a note: "You really do not expect me to pay the $50 fine levied on me. However, I will oblige you by paying these fifty potatoes. This spud's for you.—Brez."

Gomez managed for sixteen years, retiring in 2016. After the potato-ball incident, he never managed higher than Class AA. (It should be noted that Gomez was not entirely humorless. In the season's final game a few days after the potato incident, he allowed Oscar Mejia to play all nine positions.) For that same game, the Bills' general manager, Bill Terlicky, quickly crafted a promotion in which fans would get in for a dollar and a potato, with donations going to a food bank.

The potato incident didn't make page-one news back in Cleveland. (On the day of the game, the Indians were beating the Tigers in Detroit, and the big news in Cleveland was the announcement that the Higbee Company retailer was up for sale.) But Bresnahan's popularity soared. He was interviewed by media outlets all over the country, including the *Chicago Tribune*'s Bob Verdi, who, in a December 1987 column, named him Sports Person of the Year.

For a May 1988 game, the Bills—with recently appointed general manager Rick Muntean—brought back the prankster catcher for Dave Bresnahan Day. Bresnahan autographed potatoes, and the Bills retired his number 59.

Muntean had been a pretty good ballplayer in his younger days and had seen the Indians at Municipal Stadium growing up. He starred as a pitcher and third baseman for Woodrow Wilson High School in Youngstown and was scouted by the Tigers and Twins. But once, after hitting a towering home run, he ran the bases backward on a lark, leaving the scouts shaking their heads. Goofiness doesn't play well with promising careers. He attended Ohio University, at one point saying, "I was going to be the voice of the Cleveland Indians."

Years later, the Williamsport team—now the Crosscutters—issued a bobblehead in Bresnahan's likeness, with the catcher gripping, of course, a potato. In 2020, one was going for almost $300 on eBay.

What happened to the potato? One of the umpires had picked up the potato, or remnants thereof, and tossed it in a garbage can. A teenager, apparently with a savvy collector's instinct, salvaged it and put it in a specimen jar from his biology class, preserving it with denatured alcohol. He tried to offer it to the National Baseball Hall of Fame and Museum in 2000 but was referred instead to the Baseball Reliquary, where it now resides. The reliquary, a Los Angeles County Department of Arts and Culture organization, is home to artifacts that often focus on the sport's arcane moments and mementos. Its collections include a Babe Ruth partially eaten hot dog, hair curlers from Dock Ellis and other items.

Bresnahan's prank, save for a nick on his pitcher's statistical line, was harmless and taken by many in the spirit in which it was intended, save for his manager. Muntean, though, sees it as a lighthearted moment. "Baseball purists ask, 'Why? He made a travesty of the game.' But we think Dave did something that is the essence of the game—he had fun with it."

21

JOHNNY KILBANE

Cleveland's First Sports Hero

T hink LeBron James was Cleveland's first sports hero? Try Johnny Kilbane. He crafted a dynasty in boxing's featherweight division, holding the title for eleven consecutive years. When he defeated Abe Attell in 1912, he returned to an unprecedented hero's welcome, with two hundred thousand people in the streets of Cleveland.

Born in 1889, John Patrick Kilbane grew up in the "Angle," a heavily Irish area on the city's near west side. He attended St. Malachi's School. His mother died when he was three, and his father went blind when he was six, so Johnny quit school to care for his family. He gravitated to boxing at the La Salle Club, defeating a "neighborhood ruffian" named Kid Campbell. Some known boxers made their way to the club, and Kilbane was hooked. He wouldn't be the first, or the last, fighter to see the sport as a way to financial salve for his family.

A biographical feature on Kilbane, published in a Canadian newspaper days after the Cleveland celebration, describes the youngster this way: "All the time Johnny was studying boxing, often on an empty stomach. He was an apt pupil and quick to learn. It was not unusual to see him going down Detroit Street punching at imaginary figures."

Kilbane was eighteen when he had his first official fight in 1907. With a slight frame, strong jab and will to win, he found success in the ring, darting his 122-pound frame at opponents. The five-foot, five-inch Kilbane began to make a name for himself at a time when boxing's popularity in the United States was on par with what professional football would become decades later.

Johnny Kilbane. *Author's collection.*

Some discrepancies exist in Kilbane's overall record, but it's safe to say he tallied at least 142 bouts with losses in the single digits. In an era before judges' scoring, Kilbane racked up dozens of "newspaper decisions," when writers covering the fight would determine who won.

On December 23, 1911, he beat Charley White in Cleveland, and talk turned to training for a rematch or a bout with Johnny Griffith of Akron. But neither materialized, and the title fight with Attell was set for February 22 in Vernon, California.

The fight would be a rematch. Kilbane had lost a ten-round match with the champion Attell in 1910. By the time Kilbane and Attell squared off on February 22, 1912—Attell's birthday as well as George Washington's—the Cleveland native had been fighting for five years.

Kilbane's acumen in the ring was built on his "speed and skill, rather than a thundering fist. In fact, he was growing a reputation as someone lacking a knockout punch, someone who could never be a great champion," as one writer put it. In keeping with the air of confidence boxers show to this day, both predicted victory, with Kilbane definitively stating, "I am going to take the championship title back to Cleveland with me." The hometown paper openly pulled for its local boy. Four days before the fight, a headline ran over boxing writer J.P. Garvey's column in the *Plain Dealer*: "Abe Attell's Reign as Champion Featherweight Is Almost Over."

A crowd of nine thousand turned out in Vernon, a city tucked near Los Angeles that as of 2017 had seventy-six residents and is almost exclusively industrial. But more than one hundred years ago, boxing, baseball and booze were the economic drivers in Vernon, thanks to barman Jack Doyle. His open-air arena held fights on a regular basis, while his bar attracted celebrities.

Tommy Kilbane (unrelated) and Frankie Conley—two fighters Kilbane had defeated—were in his corner, along with manager Jimmy Dunn.

Kilbane and Attell battled in a fight that saw no knockdowns, but in the eighth, the Clevelander landed sixteen consecutive shots in what one account praised as a "sensational struggle." The referee's decision went to Kilbane; Attell claimed, in that traditional boxing unacceptance of defeat, that he was robbed. Kilbane earned $3,500 for his efforts (the equivalent of almost $100,000 today), while Attell took in $6,500. (Attell also had wagered $5,000 on himself, so his payday turned out to be fairly nominal.)

Back home, all of Cleveland was ecstatic. But the homecoming party would have to wait. Kilbane remained on the West Coast, eagerly exploring entertainment options. A photo shoot brought in $2,000. A San Francisco playhouse engagement lasted a week. As *Akron Beacon Journal* columnist Bob Dyer once wrote, Kilbane "was in no hurry to defend his title and take the risk of cutting off his financial geyser." But in mid-March, the trek home began. Little did Kilbane know what was in store for him.

The first inkling of the turnout actually came from a sandlot baseball league of three thousand players that enthusiastically agreed to show up to greet Kilbane on his return, scheduled for March 16. A snowstorm in Syracuse, Kansas, less than twenty miles from the Colorado border, delayed the Kilbane party for two days. Kilbane said years later that he would always remember the storm.

They trekked on, with newspapermen and photographers boarding the train in Toledo, Sandusky and Elyria. Then they arrived in Cleveland, where police had to clear the way from the train station. It wasn't even a traditional parade with a route; it was Kilbane and family going from the station to his home.

"The crowd fairly swept me from my feet. No visitor to Cleveland ever received the ovation that my fellow townsmen gave me. I have never forgotten it, and never will."

As luck would have it, with the delay, Kilbane arrived in the city on March 17, St. Patrick's Day. "The fact that he is Irish will add to the celebration," one paper reported. Cleveland was bathed in "a solid mass of green."

It was moderate for a March day in Cleveland, with a low of thirty-two degrees and a high of fifty. Six bands played in the procession. The Cleveland Naps, training in Alabama, sent a telegram. (Kilbane was friends with several players.) A two-mile-long procession was filled with people carrying flags that read "Our Johnny." The crowd clung to the coats of police officers. Reports say two hundred thousand people, with many on housetops from Detroit Avenue to West Seventy-Fifth Street, watched the procession take Kilbane, his wife, his daughter and manager Jimmy Dunn to the champion's home on Herman Avenue. Many lining the street were crying, reports said, as was Kilbane.

"When Johnny Kilbane came home to Cleveland yesterday the crowds which welcomed him were the largest yet. No president of the United States, or popular candidate for president, ever received such a welcome in

Johnny Kilbane lived at 7413 Herman Avenue. The thousands of people who showed up for his parade in 1912 wound their way to the home on Cleveland's West Side. *Marc Bona.*

Cleveland. The crowds down town were as large as four or five election night jams rolled into one."

One account, forty years later, remembers the festivities as "the greatest civic celebration ever given any man—be he athlete, soldier, statesman or hero—in the history of Cleveland."

Kilbane had endeared himself as one of the city's own, his reputation as a "clean-living lad" helping.

Newly elected mayor Newton Baker, a close pal of Kilbane's whose friendship would prove helpful later, joined the procession. (Baker's name lives on; he was a founding partner of the BakerHostetler law firm.)

A tragic moment occurred during the parade, however, when a boy, Andy Dehil, racing across Superior Avenue, was struck by a car. "Don't take me away, I want to see Johnny; he will go by and I won't see him," the boy reportedly said. A day later, Kilbane brought flowers to the hospitalized boy. Not everyone was happy with the celebration. Baptist ministers formally condemned city officials who participated in the celebration, deeming it a desecration of the Sabbath.

The aftermath of the fight saw the party continue a few days later, when Kilbane and pals were caught in a "traffic tangle" near a beer-wagon driver. For some reason, the driver decided to mouth off to the boxer. Kilbane's pals defended him, and the boxer had to play peacemaker.

As is almost always the case after a hard-fought title bout, the rumor mill churned talk of a rematch, supposedly set for Labor Day in Vernon. The match never materialized, and the two never fought each other again. Kilbane supposedly was planning to take his father to his native Ireland.

Other reports filtered as to who Kilbane would fight next—Ad Wolgast on July 4, or Johnny Dundee perhaps? It turned out to be Frankie Burns in New York on May 14 in a nontitle defense that Kilbane won. Remarkably, exactly one week later, Kilbane fought again, with the title on the line, and defeated Jimmy Walsh in Boston. Thus began a championship reign that would last until 1923.

His penchant for theater continued, too, as he signed a deal to appear at B.F. Keith's Hippodrome in Cleveland. It was the first time a fighter had "played" the theater, and friends from the La Salle boxing club showed up to support him, along with the mayor and police chief. Kilbane was offered $50,000 for a two-year contract both for boxing matches and entertainment appearances, which included the nascent movie industry.

Kilbane was, by all accounts, a family man who never forgot his Cleveland roots. He would fight two dozen times in the city, from League Park to

Gray's Armory. He also became friends with several of the Cleveland Naps, including Ray Chapman, whose major-league debut came months after the Attell-Kilbane fight. On October 27, 1919, Kilbane would be among several dignitaries at one of the biggest social events in Cleveland, Chapman's bachelor dinner at the Hotel Winton on Prospect Avenue two days before the Naps' infielder married socialite Kathleen Daly.

Kilbane's close friendship with Chapman and the fight with Attell include an interesting footnote. Attell, while a known fighter in his day (he was champion from 1906 to 1912), also was a gambler. He retired from boxing in 1917 and, two years later, was suspected of being an integral component of the World Series fix in the infamous Black Sox scandal.

The boxer and ballplayer's friendship was a pairing of two of the best-known and well-liked Cleveland athletes of their day. Kilbane was so close with Chapman that, in 1920, while on vacation in Michigan, he scrambled to get back to the city for his friend's funeral. Chapman, of course, had been infamously beaned in a game in New York and died from his injuries. Kilbane couldn't find a boat, so he rented a tug. He arrived at 4:00 a.m. and made it to the church.

A trio of statues represents Johnny Kilbane at three stages in his life: as a young boy, as a boxer and his later career as clerk of Cleveland Municipal Court. *Marc Bona.*

Johnny Kilbane is buried in Calvary Cemetery in Cleveland. *Marc Bona.*

In later years, Kilbane became a politician, losing city council and sheriff races, but he was elected to state senate and state house seats before becoming clerk of courts in Cleveland.

In 2014, Irish sculptor Rowan Gillespie installed a trio of statues honoring Kilbane in various stages, representing him as a boy, as a fighter and in post-boxing life. They stand in Battery Park, not far from the Cleveland neighborhood where Kilbane grew up.

His memory lives on in a variety of ways. Galway Bay Brewery in Ireland made A Fighting Heart Irish Ale to mark the centennial of his victory over Attell. And Cleveland's Great Lakes Brewing Company—founded by the Conway brothers, whose lineage dates to Ireland—made Fighting Heart Irish Red Ale to honor Kilbane.

When he was young, Kilbane told a close friend, Perk Gibbons, about his desire to become a boxer. His pal encouraged him to find out if fighting "is all in your heart, or maybe just in your head." The words would stay with Kilbane, who years later wrote a poem. Its final lines:

This need of heart is not just for
the pugilist who fights
But it holds true for all of us
Who battle for our rights
For when the chips of life are down
and troubled waters mount
A fighting heart will see us through
However long the count

22

THE FORGOTTEN TRAGEDY OF 1993

I n March 1993, as the Indians were holding their first spring training in Winter Haven, Florida, a tragedy shook the team: Pitchers Steve Olin and Tim Crews were killed in a boating accident. Players dying in the middle of their careers is rare; the death of teammates is even less common. Mourning and remembrances would follow one of the biggest stories in sports that year. But what is often overshadowed is that, just eight months later, tragedy would strike another pitcher on the staff.

When news broke of the boating accident, initial reports covered the death of Olin, while Crews and Bob Ojeda were seriously injured. Crews died the following day. The accident had taken place on March 22, a rare off day during spring training. The teammates decided to go bass fishing on Little Lake Nellie just west of Orlando and about forty miles north of Winter Haven. But their eighteen-foot boat slammed into a new fishing dock. The boat, with the three players still aboard, went under the dock and kept going for another one hundred feet.

"They never even knew what hit them," said Perry Brigmond, a close friend of Crews who had arrived on the scene.

Off the field, the tragedy lingered. They left wives, children, teammates. Cleveland fans were shocked, and the outpouring of grief continued. On the field, when the season began just two weeks later, the Indians had to deal with a depleted pitching staff and the emotional trauma that comes with losing friends. Charles Nagy was coming off a seventeen-win season and an All-Star appearance, but he was injured early in the year. Ojeda

The memoriam patch honoring Tim Crews and Steve Olin, the Indian pitchers who died in 1993. No one would know that later that year their teammate Cliff Young also would die tragically. *Marc Bona.*

was healing from the injuries he suffered in the accident. Several pitchers were vying for spots on the team.

The Indians played the season wearing mourning patches that the bullpen pitchers designed as a baseball emblem. Olin's number 31 had an arrow pointing up, a symbolic reminder he used to draw on the underside of the bill of his cap to throw strikes. To the right was Crews's number 52, with a star, representing how good he was, said fellow pitcher Kevin Wickander, a close friend of Olin's.

Less than two months after the accident, Wickander was traded to the Cincinnati Reds, a decision to help break the emotional trap the pitcher was in as he dealt with the deaths. The team brought up a left-handed pitcher from Class AAA Charlotte, Cliff Young.

Young had been a three-sport star at Willis High School in Texas. He had played quarterback, leading his team to a 9-2-1 record his senior season. He was a standout at basketball who had considered attending the University of Houston to play for legendary coach Guy Lewis. But he could throw a baseball ninety-two miles per hour, and in 1983, the Montreal Expos drafted him in the fifth round.

The sixth of ten children, he grew up in Willis, a town of 1,674 about forty-five miles north of Houston. He wound his way through the minor-league ranks, starting with rookie ball in 1983 in Calgary. In 1990, now with the California Angels organization, he was called up and went 1-1. A year later, he split his time between the Angels and Class AAA Edmonton, going 1-0 in the bigs. After a year back in Class AAA, he signed with the Indians on November 3, 1992, and joined the team for that ill-fated 1993 spring training. He appeared in twenty-one games for the Tribe, going 3-3 with one save. He made $125,000 that season.

But elbow problems relegated him to the bullpen, and he underwent arthroscopic surgery in August. (When Young went down, Julian Tavarez replaced him and made the first start in his seventeen-year major-league career.) The Indians limped to a lackluster 76-86 sixth-place finish.

On November 4, 1993, back home in Willis, Young was driving his 1993 Toyota 4Runner south on Old Egypt Road just west of I-45 about 9:30

Cleveland Indian pitcher Steve Olin, in an older jersey. *Nancy Stone, the Plain Dealer.*

p.m. He was with a former basketball pal, John Wilkerson, and they were driving to pick up Young's wife, Tamara, at work. Suddenly, his car veered off the winding road and slammed into a tree. Wilkerson later told the state police that his friend was reaching to light a cigarette. The impact of the crash sent Young partially through the sunroof. The driver's side of his 4Runner was crumpled.

When her husband didn't show, Tamara caught a ride. On the way home, she saw the wreckage.

Young, not wearing a seat belt, was killed instantly. Coverage of the accident included a lead paragraph in a Texas newspaper that summed up the emotions in Cleveland: "For the Cleveland Indians, the mourning resumes."

As the cliché goes, everyone knows everyone, for better or worse, in a small town. In the coming days, Young was remembered fondly in so many ways from so many people.

About six hundred people attended a remembrance at his high school. When a highlight reel played showing Young with the Indians, many attendees, overcome by grief, had to be escorted out of the service.

"I remember him coming out to practice and not having enough money to eat. Here was a poor kid who had the opportunity and took it. He was a great competitor. Cliff was the first one to make it….Cliff kind of opened the door and showed that it was possible," said Danny Freeman, who coached baseball and football at the school.

Young was remembered as a lover of animals and the outdoors and a person who never forgot where he came from. He and Tamara, who had known each other since grade school, were high school sweethearts and married in 1987. They had two young boys. He lived a mile from his high school.

"The hurt and grief is inexplicable," Reverend Leroy Thompson told the mourners.

"He had a lot of love in his heart for the game and people. We'll miss him," said Indian manager Mike Hargrove, who by all accounts did an admirable job holding together a ball club reeling from the loss of Crews and Olin. He attended the funeral along with Kenny Lofton and Ojeda.

"On the heels of what happened in spring training, this tragic event comes as even a greater shock to our organization," Indian general manager John Hart said.

"Cliff was the kind of guy who would go out and pitch a two-hit shutout and then apologize for giving up those two hits," said Charlie Manuel, who managed Young in Charlotte and who later became the Indians' skipper.

Mike Hargrove in 1993. The Indians' manager deftly guided his team dealing with the emotional toll from the deaths of teammates. *James A. Ross, the Plain Dealer.*

Young was shy about asking salesmen for equipment or shoes, said his agent, Phil Tannenbaum. Tannenbaum—who said a signed deal was in place to bring back Young for the coming season—said the pitcher tried to do everything he could to help the families of Crews and Olin, even though at that point in his career he had known them only a few weeks.

Patti Olin, Steve's widow, also flew to Texas for the funeral, where an Indian jersey hung among floral wreaths.

Less than two weeks after Young's death, the Indians established a memorial fund for the pitcher's children.

The year 1993 will be remembered for many losses in the sports world, among them North Carolina State basketball coach Jim Valvano of cancer, tennis star and civil-rights advocate Arthur Ashe from AIDS, Boston Celtic Reggie Lewis of a heart attack, Croatian basketball star and NBA standout Drazen Petrovic in a car accident and the Zambian national soccer team in a plane crash.

Young's death brought back the memories of Olin and Crews, Hart said at the time. "I had that same heart-wrenching feeling of sorrow and helplessness. We are looking forward to calendar year 1993 going away. You just shake your head and you wonder, 'Why is this happening?'"

Five days after he died, in the aftermath of the coverage of his death, an editorial about Young appeared in the *Plain Dealer*. It ended with this observation: "Cleveland hardly knew Cliff Young, which is sad, because he seemed like a man worth knowing."

23

PELÉ AND CLEVELAND

S occer has gained a foothold in the United States, but it took decades, and it's still light-years behind European and South American teams and leagues.

It's not for lack of trying. In the 1960s, professional leagues cropped up in the United States. Without an established farm system, a league was started with almost exclusively imported players. The United Soccer Association, which began play in 1967, used a "lend-lease arrangement" to bring in players. The teams in American cities took on an almost sister-city arrangement with their foreign locales. Cleveland's partner was Stoke-on-Trent, more than 150 miles northwest of London.

The arrangement included clubs in the United Kingdom, Brazil, Holland, Italy and Uruguay. Initially, a twelve-team circuit was organized.

The Cleveland Stokers began play with well-known owners but not-so-well-known players—at least not to an American audience. Cleveland Indian owner Vernon Stouffer and general manager Gabe Paul led the ownership team in 1967. In 1968, the Stokers joined the North American Soccer League, formed from a merger between the United Soccer Association and the National Professional Soccer League. Politician Howard Metzenbaum and Ted Bonda, who would become president of the Indians, were added to the ownership ranks.

The Stokers finished 5-3-4 in their inaugural season and 14-7-11 in 1968, their second—and final—year.

The Cleveland Stokers hosted Los Angeles on April 21, 1968. The team took its name from an English city club. *Robert J. Quinlan, the Plain Dealer.*

The Stokers wore red-and-white-striped uniforms, similar to their UK counterparts. Their melting-pot roster pulled from eleven countries, with only one native North American on the roster. The team made John Mueller the only American-born and first high school player to be picked in the draft. Ironically, Mueller had attended Cleveland High School in St. Louis.

Richard Skora was the first player to sign with the Stokers. The German-born player had graduated from Lincoln High School in 1964 and was believed to be the "finest soccer player in the Cleveland area."

Early on, there was talk of a television deal. Stoker business manager Marsh Samuel said the team was trying to arrange a broadcast deal for road games. But that idea faced competition from baseball's comfortable, and established, visuals on the tube.

What the Stokers had, though, was a "small but intensely loyal following," thanks in part to WXEN's coverage. The local station was small but focused on programming for people of different nationalities. Average attendance the first year was 6,507. It dropped to 4,305 in 1968. With one exception, attendance never exceeded 10,000, which resulted "in a lot of rattling" in the cavernous Cleveland Municipal Stadium.

Pelé, shown when he played for the New York Cosmos. Arguably the greatest soccer player ever, his teams won often, but not on a July 1968 night at Cleveland Municipal Stadium. *George Heinz, the Plain Dealer.*

The one exception came on July 10, 1968. That night, Santos, a dominant Brazilian team, came to Cleveland as part of a North American tour, playing "friendlys" (exhibitions). The team was loaded with stars, but none shined brighter than a five-foot, eight-inch, twenty-seven-year-old prolific goal scorer named Edson Arantes do Nascimento—better known as Pelé.

Even American non-soccer fans knew who Pelé was. His salary was as well known as his prowess on a soccer pitch. He made close to $1 million (actually about $800,000), a statistic that was repeated and even printed in ads touting the game. Some outlets even noted that the money was tax-free.

How good were Santos and Pelé? Between 1957 and 1962, during a stretch of 456 games, Santos and the Brazilian national team for which Pelé also played did not lose. In the low-scoring sport, he had scored eight goals in a single game once, five goals four times and four goals eighteen times. This, despite opponents double- and triple-teaming him routinely.

Opponents lauded Pelé's abilities as well as those of the team. "They can read each other's minds. They don't even need to look before they pass. They know exactly where a man is going to be and then—poof," said Kansas City's Ernie Winchester, whose team had been beaten, 4–1, by Santos a week before the Cleveland game. Gerd Wiedemeir, who had to try to defend Pelé in that game, said, "He is the best I've ever seen. His speed, his technique." Wiedemeir reportedly turned up his palms to the reporter, finding no other words to describe the man known as the "King of Soccer."

The Santos-Stokers game was heavily publicized. The Stokers had to pay $27,500 to bring in the stellar Brazilian squad. Both teams were coming off wins. The Stokers had edged Dallas, 2–1, four days earlier. On July 8, Santos had beaten Boston, the Brazilian team's seventh consecutive win on its North American tour.

Timing was good for the game. Baseball was in its midsummer break for the All-Star Game, held the previous night in Houston. The National League won, 1–0, with Cleveland's Luis Tiant taking the loss. Sam McDowell struck out Willie Mays. Also in baseball news: The day of the soccer game, Baltimore Oriole manager Hank Bauer was fired, ushering in Earl Weaver's eighteen-year tenure as skipper, during which he managed more than 2,500 games. The sports world, though, was still reeling from the official announcement from the NBA about the Wilt Chamberlain trade, one of the most monumental in basketball history. On July 9, 1968, the Philadelphia 76ers had dealt Chamberlain to the Los Angeles Lakers for center Darrall Imhoff, forward Jerry Chambers and guard Archie Clark.

But on July 10, a seasonal summer night in Cleveland, fans were thinking soccer. Upper-box tickets cost five dollars, upper reserved went for four dollars, lower deck ran three dollars and bleachers cost a buck. Promotional coverage touted "no increase in prices for this international match." Kickoff was set for 8:00 p.m., and 16,205 fans turned out, the most for a soccer game in Cleveland. Before the game, flags and flowers were exchanged in a diplomatic courtesy.

Cleveland drew first blood when Spanish striker Enrique Mateos put a penalty kick past Santos goalkeeper Laércio at the 26:30 mark of the first half. The Brazilians, with their roster chock full of one-named players, evened the score almost six minutes into the second half when Pelé crossed to Covaldo, who passed to Toninho, who chest-bumped the ball past Cleveland goalie Paul Shardlow. The Stokers then regained the lead after Dietrich Albrecht and Laércio raced after a ball, with the Cleveland player beating the goaltender and kicking into an open net.

Then, with 1:12 remaining in the game, Toninho shot a ball past Shardlow. The Brazilian celebration at apparently earning a draw was quelled immediately: The officials ruled the play offside. Referee Henry

The 1968 Cleveland Stokers included goaltender Paul Shardlow *(fifth from the left, back row)*. *Andrew Cifranic, the Plain Dealer.*

Landauer said he had seen linesman Jack Connor with his hand up for the infraction and "I knew immediately I would disallow the call."

Offside in soccer is tricky, because, unlike hockey, there is no set line on the field of play demarcating the illegal area. It is a moving line.

Coverage of the game tabbed the decision as nearly causing a riot— seemingly a lot of hyperbole, considering the fans were cheering for Cleveland. But Santos players were beside themselves. Connor was kicked in the shins. Brazilian players jumped on top of the field tarp, rolled up by the third-base dugout, and argued with fans. Pelé spit at the crowd. A dozen cops came onto the field to keep the peace. A small band quickly started playing music in an attempt to calm things during the turbulent moments, much like orchestra members playing as the *Titanic* sank.

The remaining seventy-two seconds were never played, because Santos, the officials noted, "debated their time away," Landauer said. It was a belligerent ending to the game, but still a win for the Clevelanders.

The officials were escorted out in a police car, and most of the Cleveland players thought the call was wrong. Afterward, Stoker coach Herman Low said he did not know if the play was offside.

Coverage of the game credits the Stokers with keeping Santos in check all night. "The Santos players were forced to shoot from far range, it wasn't their game. Santos was sluggish and its attacks were sporadic forays." Pelé was scoreless in ten shots. He was marked by Ruben Navarro, who Pelé called the greatest defender he had ever faced. And Shardlow's block of a penalty kick from Toninho was called a "one in 1,000 diving stop" that drew a huge roar from the hometown faithful. Another story described the goaltender as "cat-like," saying he "made diving save after save, from the feet of Santos' best, Pelé, Pepe and Toninho."

Almost immediately, Santos called for a rematch, which the Stokers accepted. The teams agreed on a date, August 5. It was a travel day for the Indians, so the stadium would be empty and fans would not have baseball as a competitive distraction. But after the July 10 game and before the rematch could be played, Pelé was injured during a game in Uruguay, forcing the cancellation of several of Santos's games, including the sequel against Cleveland.

The attendance figure boosted the confidence of the Stokers' ownership to declare that the team would return in 1969. One writer declared: "If we had drawn only our usual 4,000 to 5,000 spectators, we'd have known that we have only 5,000 soccer fans in Cleveland. Now, we know that at least 16,000 have enough interest to come out at least on occasion." The problem with that premature logic was that the "occasion" had brought the world's greatest player to the shores of Lake Erie.

Two months later, the season ended. The league went on, but the Stokers didn't. The fan base wasn't there long-term.

Weeks after the season, Shardlow was training with Stoke City. He collapsed and died of a suspected heart attack. He was twenty-five. His finest hour, Dan Coughlin of the *Plain Dealer* wrote in the announcement of Shardlow's death, came on July 10, 1968, with his stellar play against Pelé and Santos.

On September 1, 1976, Pelé, now with the New York Cosmos, returned to Cleveland on a rainy night for a neutral-site game against the Dallas Tornado. A more-than-respectable crowd of 14,119 showed up for the 2–2 draw. Pelé played all ninety minutes in the game, which was void of controversy. Like the game eight years earlier, he did not score.

24

LUKE EASTER

A Memorable Home Run, a Tragic Ending

In 1952, Barnard Malamud came out with *The Natural*, a book about a ballplayer with God-given abilities whose career takes on mythical proportions. In 1984, the movie of the same name was released starring Robert Redford as Roy Hobbs, whose home runs become legendary smashes. It's been said that real-life ballplayer Eddie Waitkus served as an inspiration for Malamud's book. Waitkus was a tragic hero, having been shot by a young woman in June 1949. He eventually recovered and went on to play until 1955.

Eight days before Eddie Waitkus Day was held at Shibe Park in Philadelphia on August 19, 1949, and three years prior to the book's release, Luke Easter made his big-league debut with the Cleveland Indians. He was the eleventh player to break Major League Baseball's color barrier in the twentieth century since Jackie Robinson began his career with the Brooklyn Dodgers in 1947. Throughout his career, Easter's age was always a bit fuzzy, difficult to nail down with accuracy. What wasn't unclear was his ability to hit prodigious home runs that had writers scrambling to guesstimate distances before the term *tape-measure home run* was used.

He was born Luscious Easter in what turned out to be 1915 in Mississippi. While working for the Titanium Pigment Company, he began earning a few bucks playing for the company's ball club. He moved to the Negro Leagues, where, in his debut for the Homestead Grays in May 1947, he slammed a ball 435 feet for his first home run. He finished the season with fifty-six home runs. He then played for the Pacific Coast League's San Diego Padres.

Long before the Home Run Derby was a thing, the team began scheduling early batting practice so folks could watch Easter's monumental clouts. (One of the many kids who lined up at the park to watch Easter take batting practice was a young Frank Robinson, who would grow up to have his own storied career as a player and a manager with the Indians.) Easter signed with the Indians in 1949, the start of what would become a six-year career. Easter had his best season in 1950. He batted .280 with 151 hits, twenty-eight home runs and 107 RBI. On June 23, 1950, Easter—a big man at six feet, four inches and 240 pounds—made his mark with a tremendous shot in Cleveland Municipal Stadium.

The Indians were playing the Washington Senators in the opener of a four-game series. Easter, batting third in the lineup ahead of cleanup hitter Larry Doby, strode to the plate with two outs in the bottom of the sixth inning before more than 26,600 fans. The big first baseman already had hit a home run in the third inning off Bob Ross. With Dale Mitchell on second, Easter faced Joe Haynes, a "right-handed curve ball specialist." Easter, a left-handed hitter, dug in, rocketing Haynes's 3-0 pitch into the upper right-field stands. The "bazooka blast," as it was recorded in the *Plain Dealer*, was estimated to have traveled 470 feet. Folks from Case Institute of Technology later determined the distance at 477 feet. Either way, Easter, the newspaper reported, had "clouted what is generally considered to be the longest home run ever hit in major league competition at the lakefront arena." It landed in the box seats of Section 4. Easter finished the day 2-4 with a walk, three runs scored and six RBIs. But it was the moonshot off of Haynes that people would remember. (On August 1, 1951, Easter faced Haynes again, this time in Washington, and he hit another home run.)

Easter and Haynes did not know it then, but they would be bound by tragic endings.

At the time of Easter's blast, Haynes was nearing the end of his career. He had married into a baseball family. In 1941, he wed Thelma Griffith, personal secretary and niece of the Washington Senators' owner, Calvin Griffith. In 1948, the Chicago White Sox traded Haynes to Cleveland, but he never played for the Indians; a month later, he was dealt to Washington for Mickey Vernon and Early Wynn. He retired in 1952 and became the Senators' minor-league pitching instructor a few years later. He moved up to executive vice-president, a role he kept when the Senators moved to Minneapolis–St. Paul. He lived with his family in Hopkins, a suburb about ten miles from the Twin Cities. On January 6, 1967, Haynes suffered a fatal heart attack while shoveling snow. He was forty-nine.

Indian catcher Jim Hegan congratulates Bob Feller, who is carried off the field by teammates Al Rosen (*left*) and Luke Easter after earning his twentieth victory of the 1951 season. Easter and Rosen in particular were close pals. *Plain Dealer file photo.*

Easter's final major-league season was 1954, but he would play another decade in minor-league ball, continuing to hit his legendary home runs. His biographer, Alex Painter, logged 650 home runs Easter hit from 1946 to 1964 in professional baseball.

Easter made his post-career home in Cleveland. He had invested in Ray's Sausage in 1953, an East Side business that still exists, as well as in a popular jazz club. He became chief union steward with the aircraft workers alliance at TRW. His fellow employees trusted him with the task of cashing their paychecks every other Thursday. Usually, with a bag full of money, he had a police escort. But not on March 29, 1979.

Easter had left the Cleveland Trust Bank branch at 260th Street and Euclid Avenue with about $40,000. What happened next sounds like a scene from a television show or a movie.

Two men, Victor L. Pritchett and Roderick C. Thomas, confronted him. One had a revolver, the other a shotgun. Both had police records. Easter was shot, with the fatal bullet coming from the revolver held by Pritchett, the court later found.

Pritchett and Thomas raced several miles to the west before crashing into a bridge abutment at East 140th Street and Aspinwall Avenue. The suspects fired at a police car; the officers jumped out and shot back. The suspect who had driven the getaway car ran, fell and was caught. His accomplice tried to escape in a motorist's car, which he ended up using as a shield as he shot at police. The driver of the car lay down in his vehicle during the shooting. The shooter then gave up. No one was hurt. Both suspects were found with money shoved into their pockets. Because the men fired at police, they were charged with multiple attempted-murder charges. It was a good bet the men knew about Easter's cash-carrying arrangement. A year earlier, Thomas had been fired by TRW.

Three months later, Thomas was found guilty of aggravated murder, aggravated robbery and three counts of attempted murder. He was sentenced to life plus additional consecutive terms. Pritchett's trial came later. He pled guilty, was sentenced to fifteen years to life and died in prison in 1995. As of 2014, Thomas was still in prison.

Easter was laid to rest on April 3, 1979. Before Mount Sinai Baptist Church filled with mourners remembering an easygoing, friendly man, there were remembrances at a nearby funeral home. So popular was the former slugger that calling hours were extended to accommodate more than four thousand people who paid respects.

Bob Feller attended, and Mayor Dennis Kucinich showed up. Former players serving as pallbearers included Al Rosen, who had been teammates with Easter. The two were pals in their playing days. Easter, once so excited at seeing Rosen hit a home run, jumped up in the dugout and knocked himself out on the cement roof as he cheered for his friend. Bob Cain, a pitcher who played at the same time, also was a pallbearer. Cain never played for Cleveland, but he lived in Euclid. (Cain apparently had the proverbial soft spot in his heart. In 1951, he was the pitcher who threw to midget Eddie Gaedel, whose brief career was orchestrated as a short-lived stunt from the St. Louis Browns' owner, Bill Veeck. When Gaedel died in 1961, Cain was the only person from baseball to attend the one-at-bat Gaedel's funeral.)

Easter was remembered fondly. "He had a marvelous ability to get along with people and make them feel important," said John O. Cantlay, a TRW manager.

Luke Easter's memory lives. In 1900, the City of Cleveland acquired land at Kinsman Road and East 116th Street. It featured woods, a creek, a dance

Luke Easter is buried in Highland Park Cemetery in Highland Hills, Ohio. *Marc Bona.*

hall and even a tiny airport for early mail flights for a couple of years. It evolved into a neighborhood recreational center. A skating rink, courts and sports fields—including ten baseball diamonds—were added. It became a gathering place for many African Americans who lived in the area.

In 1980, it was renamed Luke Easter Park.

BIBLIOGRAPHY

Newspapers Accessed Online

Akron Beacon Journal
Alabama Tribune (Montgomery)
Anniston (AL) Star
Asbury Park (NJ) Press
Baltimore Sun
Binghamton (NY) Press and Sun-Bulletin
Boston Globe
Bridgeport (CT) Times and Evening Farmer
Buffalo Enquirer
Chicago Tribune
Cincinnati Enquirer
Cleveland Jewish News
Courier Post (Camden, NJ)
Daily Reporter (Dover, OH)
Daily Republican-Register (Mt. Carmel, IL)
Daily Times (New Philadelphia, OH)
Davis Reflex-Journal (Bountiful, UT)
Dayton (OH) Daily News
Detroit Free Press
Dothan (AL) Eagle
Eugene (OR) Register-Guard

Evansville (IN) Press
Evening Independent (Massillon, OH)
Evening Review (East Liverpool, OH)
Evening Sun (Baltimore, MD)
Evening Times (Sayre, PA)
Fall River (MA) Daily Evening News
Forest Republican (Tionesta, PA)
Gazette (Cedar Rapids, IA)
Hartford Courant
Indianapolis Star
Kansas City Star
Keyport (NJ) Weekly
Los Angeles Times
Medina (OH) Gazette
Miami Herald
Monitor (McAllen, TX)
Newsday
News-Herald (Franklin, PA)
News-Herald (Willoughby, OH)
News Journal (Mansfield, OH)
New York Daily News
New York Times
Odessa (TX) American
Orlando Sentinel
Ottawa Citizen
Philadelphia Inquirer
Pittsburgh Daily Post
Pittsburgh Post-Gazette
Pittsburgh Press
Pittsburgh Sun-Telegraph
Plain Dealer (Cleveland)
Portsmouth (OH) Daily Times
Record (Hackensack, NJ)
Salt Lake Tribune
Sandusky (OH) Star-Journal
Shelbina (MO) Democrat
St. Louis Globe Democrat
St. Louis Post-Dispatch
Southern Illinoisan (Carbondale, IL)

Standard Speaker (Hazleton, PA)
Star Beacon (Ashtabula, OH)
Star Press (Muncie, IN)
Star Tribune (Minneapolis, MN)
Tampa Bay Newspapers
Times-Picayune
Tribune (Scranton, PA)
Tribune Chronicle (Warren, OH)
Washington Herald
Washington Post
Wilkes-Barre (PA) Times Leader
Windsor (Canada) Star
Winnipeg (Canada) Tribune
Xenia (OH) Daily Gazette
York (PA) Daily

Books

Alexander, Charles C. *Spoke: A Biography of Tris Speaker*. Dallas: Southern Methodist University Press, 2007.

Austin, Dan. *Baseball's Last Great Scout*. Lincoln: University of Nebraska Press, 2013.

Bowden, Mark. *Road Work: Among Tyrants, Heroes, Rogues, and Beasts*. New York: Grove Press, 2004.

Clemons, Clarence, and Don Reo. *Big Man: Real Life & Tall Tales*. New York: Grand Central, 2010.

Conner, Floyd. *Baseball's Most Wanted*. Lincoln, NE: Potomac Books, 2002.

Dickson, Paul. *Bill Veeck: Baseball's Great Maverick*. New York: Walker & Company, 2012.

———. *The Dickson Baseball Dictionary*. New York: W.W. Norton, 1989.

Dyer, Bob. *The Top 20 Moments in Cleveland Sports*. Cleveland, OH: Gray & Company, 2007.

Egan Jr., James. *Base Ball on the Western Reserve*. Jefferson, NC: McFarland, 2008.

Enders, Eric. *Ballparks: Then and Now*. San Diego, CA: Thunder Bay Press, 2002.

Evans, Billy. *Umpiring from the Inside*. N.p.: self-published, 1947.

Feller, Bob. *Pitching to Win*. New York: Grosset & Dunlap, 1948.

Griffith, R.D. *To the NFL*. Mustang, OK: Tate Publishing, 2014.

Hatfield, Thomas. *The History of Soccer in Greater Cleveland from 1906 until 1981*. Denver, CO: Outskirts Press, 2014.

Heisman, John M., and Mark Schlabach. *John Heisman: The Man Behind the Trophy*. New York: Howard Books, 2012.

Inquiry into Professional Sports: Hearings Before the House Select Committee. Ninety-Fourth Congress, Second Session. Washington, DC: U.S. Government Printing Office, 1976.

Kashatus, William C., *Diamonds in the Coalfield*. Jefferson, NC: McFarland, 2010.

Krsolovic, Ken, and Bryan Fritz. *League Park: 1891–1946*. Jefferson, NC: McFarland, 2013.

Longert, Scott. *The Best They Could Be*. Washington, DC: Potomac Books, 2013.

Madden, Bill. *George Steinbrenner: The Last Lion of Baseball*. New York: HarperCollins, 2010.

Miller, John J. *The Big Scrum*. New York: Harper Perennial, 2011.

Mitchell, Eddie. *Baseball Rowdies of the 20th Century*. Jefferson, NC: McFarland, 2018.

Nemec, David. *Major League Baseball Profiles, 1871–1900*. Vol. 2. Lincoln: University of Nebraska Press, 2011.

Painter, Alex. *Folk Hero Forever*. Columbia, SC: Lulu, 2018.

Piascik, Andy. *The Best Show in Football: The 1946–1955 Cleveland Browns—Pro Football's Greatest Dynasty*. Taylor Trade Publications, 2012.

Pluto, Terry. *When All the World Was Browns Town*. New York: Simon & Schuster, 1997.

Podoll, Brian A. *The Minor League Milwaukee Brewers, 1859–1952*. Jefferson, NC: McFarland, 2003.

Ross, Robert B. *The Great Baseball Revolt*. Lincoln: University of Nebraska Press, 2016.

Schneider, Russell. *The Cleveland Indians Encyclopedia*. Champaign, IL: Sports Publishing, 1996.

Schwartz, Ted. *Shocking Stories of the Cleveland Mob*. Charleston, SC: Arcadia Publishing, 2010.

Sowell, Mike. *The Pitch That Killed*. New York: Macmillan, 1989.

Sulecki, James C. *The Cleveland Rams: The NFL Champs Who Left Too Soon, 1936–1945*. Jefferson, NC: McFarland, 2016.

Ward, David. *Searching for My Hockey Hero*. Toronto, Canada: ECW Press, 2014.

Webster, Gary. *Tris Speaker and the 1920 Indians*. Jefferson, NC: McFarland, 2012.

Whittingham, Richard. *Rites of Autumn*. New York: Free Press, 2001.

Interviews/Correspondence

Jason Chaimovitch
Pat Conway
Mark Dukes
Duey Graham
Vince Guerrieri
Dave Hanson
Jonathon Jackson
Bill Marting
Jay Noble
Alex Painter
Rich Passan
Robert B. Ross
Mike Vaccaro
Scott Wargo

Websites

Abernathy. abernathymagazine.com.
Access Genealogy. accessgenealogy.com.
The American Hockey League. theahl.com.
BakerHostetler. bakerlaw.com.
Baraboo (WI) Public Library. baraboopubliclibrary.org.
Baseball Almanac. baseball-almanac.com.
Baseball History Daily. baseballhistorydaily.com.
Baseball Reference. baseball-reference.com.
Baseball Roundtable Baseball Reliquary. baseballroundtable.com/the-
    baseball-reliquary.
Baseball's Greatest Sacrifice. baseballsgreatestsacrifice.com.
Basketball Reference. basketball-reference.com.
Bellevue (OH) Historical Society. bellevuehistoricalsociety.com.
Bleacher Report. bleacherreport.com.
Board Game Geek. boardgamegeek.com.
Boxing Records Archive. boxrec.com.
Brainerd (MN) International Raceway. brainerdraceway.com.
Brew Cabin. brewcabin.com.
Case Text. casetext.com.

Case Western Reserve University, Encyclopedia of Cleveland History. case.
    edu/ech.

Centers for Disease Control. cdc.gov.

Cleveland.com. cleveland.com.

The Cleveland Fan. tcf.danwismar.com/about-us.1.html.

Cleveland Magazine. clevelandmagazine.com.

Cleveland 101. cleveland101.com.

Cleveland Rams. clevelandrams.com.

Cleveland Seniors. clevelandseniors.com.

CNY Central. cnycentral.com.

Cool History of Cleveland. coolhistoryofcleveland.wordpress.com.

Crain's Cleveland Business. crainscleveland.com.

The Daily Beast. thedailybeast.com.

Data USA. datausa.io.

Dayton Triangles. daytontriangles.com.

Did The Tribe Win Last Night? didthetribewinlastnight.com.

Ebay. ebay.com.

Enchanted America. enchantedamerica.wordpress.com.

ESPN. ESPN.com.

Ethan Lewis. ethanlewis.org.

Fox Sports. foxsports.com.

Golden Football Rankings. goldenrankings.com.

Greater Cleveland Sports Hall of Fame. clevelandsportshall.com.

Gridiron Gentlemen. gridirongentlemen.com.

History Channel. history.com.

The Internet Hockey Database. hockeydb.com.

Internet Movie Database. imdb.com.

Jelle's WW2 Centre. normandytothebulge.be.

Johnny Kilbane. johnnykilbane.com.

League Park. leagueparkinfo.com.

Legacy.com. legacy.com.

Living Heritage Program. livingheritage.weebly.com.

Louie B. Nunn Center for Oral History University of Kentucky Libraries.
    kentuckyoralhistory.org.

Maclean's magazine. macleans.ca.

Mountain Home: Pennsylvania and the New York Finger Lakes.
    mountainhomemag.com.

National Baseball Hall of Fame. baseballhall.org.

NBC Sports. nbcsports.com.

bibliography

Newspapers.com. newspapers.com.

The Oatcake Archives. theoatcake.wordpress.com.

Ohio Basketball Hall of Fame. ohiobasketballhalloffame.org.

Ohio City History. ohiocityhistory.com.

Ohio History Central. ohiohistorycentral.org.

125 Moments. University of Notre Dame. 125.nd.edu.

Our Game, John Thorn. ourgame.mlblogs.com.

Peach Basket Society. peachbasketsociety.blogspot.com.

The Philly Soccer Page. phillysoccerpage.net.

Pro Football Hall of Fame. profootballhof.com.

Richmond Times-Dispatch. richmond.com.

The Ringer. theringer.com.

Rolling Stone magazine. rollingstone.com.

Rowan Gillispie. rowangillespienet.files.wordpress.com.

Rutgers University. scarletknights.com.

Sharp Football Analysis. sharpfootballanalysis.com.

SLM Media Group, St. Louis. stlmag.com.

Smithsonian Magazine. smithsonianmag.com.

Society for American Baseball Research. sabr.org.

SportsBlogs Nation sbnation.com.

Sports Collectors Daily. sportscollectorsdaily.com.

Sports Encyclopedia. sportsencyclopedia.com.

Sports Illustrated. si.com.

Sports Reference. sports-reference.com.

Spotrac. spotrac.com.

Stats Crew. statscrew.com.

Stew Thornley. stewthornley.net.

St. Louis Post-Dispatch. stltoday.com.

Third String Goalie. thirdstringgoalie.blogspot.com.

University of Maryland Eastern Shore. umes.edu.

US Inflation Calculator. usinflationcalculator.com.

Watchtower Online Library. wol.jw.org.

WJW Fox 8, Cleveland. fox8.com.

World History Encyclopedia. ancient.eu.

World Hockey Association. whahockey.com.

World Sports Logos. worldsportslogos.com.

Other Research/Sources/Publications

Associated Press
Canadian Press
The Gas Age, via Google Books
Hearst's Magazine, *The World To-Day*
International News Service
The National Magazine (Cleveland): A Monthly Journal of American History,
     via Google Books
United Press International

About the Author

M arc Bona is a features writer for cleveland.com who previously worked in assorted editing roles for the *Plain Dealer* in Cleveland; the *Post-Tribune* in Gary, Indiana; the *Times Union* in Albany, New York; the *Detroit News*; the *San Antonio Light*; and the *Dallas Morning News*. Winner of numerous Cleveland Press Club writing awards, his football-based novel *The Game Changer* was published in 2018. A graduate of the University of Iowa, he lives in Akron with his wife, Lynne Sherwin, and their rescue pup, Addie. He can be reached at mbona30@neo.rr.com.

Visit us at
www.historypress.com
···